DOR
TALES
OF MYSTERY & MURDER

Roger Evans

COUNTRYSIDE BOOKS
NEWBURY BERKSHIRE

First published 2012

COUNTRYSIDE BOOKS
3 Catherine Road
Newbury, Berkshire

To view our complete range of books,
please visit us at
www.countrysidebooks.co.uk

ISBN 978 1 84674 297 2

Dedicated to the memory of
David George Fry
1955–2011
A true Dorset countryman
who loved a good story

Designed by Peter Davies, Nautilus Design
Produced through MRM Associates Ltd., Reading
Typeset by Mac Style, Beverley, E. Yorkshire
Printed by Berforts Information Press, Oxford

Contents

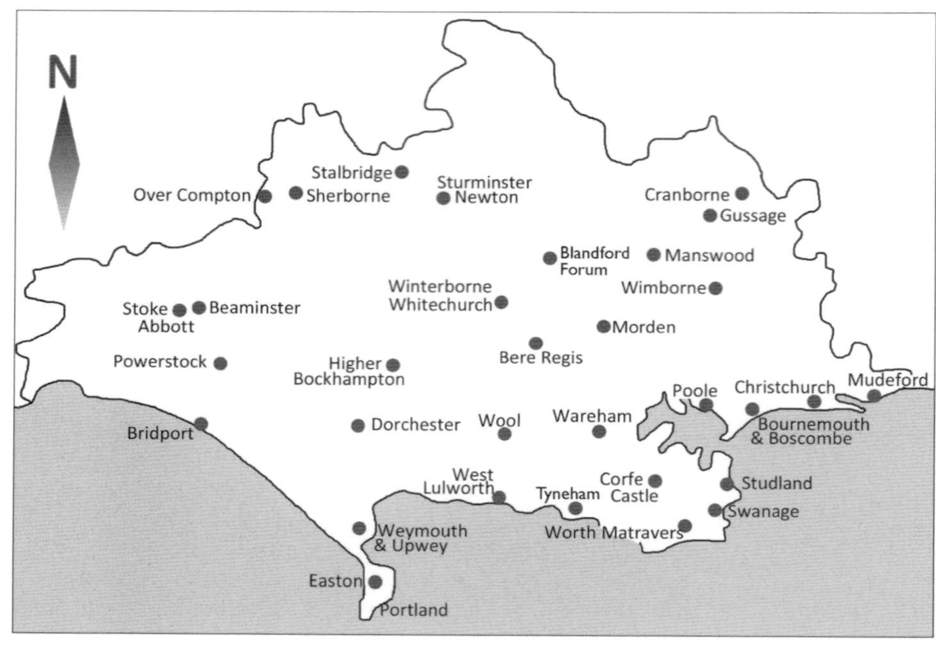

Map of Dorset showing locations of the stories

INTRODUCTION

The gently rolling hills of Dorset, the soft West Country tones of its natives, the quiet country lanes, all suggest a place where life approaches perfection. But scratch the surface and beneath lies a catalogue of mysteries and murders across the whole social spectrum. We discover a humble carter murdered by his wife; another husband whose Oxo was fatally laced with arsenic; an architect of international renown, murdered by his jealous chauffeur. We uncover the tales of two serial killers, one who bit the nipples off his victims and another who left clumps of other women's hair clenched in the hands of his victims.

Murders in Dorset were once so thick on the ground that execution days could be blessed with multiple hangings and most of them on full public display, to the amusement of massive crowds of spectators. Even Thomas Hardy witnessed the last man and the last woman to be publicly executed in the county.

Why such a rural idyllic county as Dorset should be blessed with so many murders is a mystery in itself.

Roger Evans

Thomas Hardy Watched Them Hang

Thomas Hardy, the famous author of the Wessex novels, was 86 years old when he wrote that he could 'remember what a fine figure she showed against the sky as she swung in the misty rain and how the tight, black silk gown set off her shape as she wheeled half round and back'. He was describing the execution of middle-aged Martha Brown, the last woman to be publicly executed in Dorset, an execution he had witnessed as a sixteen-year-old lad.

On leaving school, Hardy was articled to John Hicks who ran an architect's office in Dorchester's North Square. It was here, outside the prison gates, that the public executions took place. It was right on the doorstep of the office where the young Hardy worked. He was one of a crowd of 3,000 spectators. To recall the occasion in such fine detail demonstrates just how much the vision haunted him for a full 70 years. It was a vision which was no doubt the inspiration for his novel, *Tess of the d'Urbervilles*. Although the memory lingered throughout his life, it was his next experience which changed his attitude to public hangings.

Two years later, aged eighteen, the young Thomas Hardy witnessed a further execution. He rose early, read for an hour or two and then took breakfast. He had almost forgotten that there was to be an execution at 8 o'clock that morning. He raced from his home in Higher Bockhampton to reach the viewpoint high on the heath overlooking the prison. Using his brass telescope, a family heirloom, he was just in time to see James Seale drop. The lighting conditions were perfect. The sun was behind him, shining directly onto the front of the prison and the execution scene. Although Hardy viewed this from a distance of three miles, the experience disturbed him more than his first viewing, despite the first being a woman and the second being at a distance.

These events took place in 1856 and 1858, yet in 1908, when Hardy was serving as a magistrate, according to Michael Millgate's biography of Hardy, he wrote, '*As an acting Magistrate I think Capital Punishment operates as a deterrent from deliberate crimes against life to an extent that no other form of punishment can rival. But the question of the moral right of the community to inflict that punishment is one I cannot enter into in a necessarily brief communication.*'

In 1868, Victorian attitudes of decency prevailed and public executions came to an end; future hangings were executed within the confines of the prison system. Unbeknown to Hardy at the time, he had witnessed Dorset's last male and last female public hangings.

Martha Brown

It was Boxing Day in 1831 when 20-year-old Martha Brown married 39-year-old Bernard Bearn at the parish church in Powerstock. Bearn was nineteen years older than Martha and had married ten years before but his first wife had died. The newly-weds lived at a house called Meadways but fate was about to deal them a cruel hand. Two children were born but both died in infancy, within days of each other. Within months, a son from Bearn's first marriage also died aged just eleven. While Martha was still in her thirties, her husband then died and she was left a childless widow.

She took up employment as a housekeeper to the brothers John and Robert Symes, who lived at Blackmanston Farm, near Steeple, about eight miles from Swanage. She had been there several years when the 6 ft tall, 19-year-old John Brown joined the farm as a shepherd. Despite Martha being twice his age, they fell for each other and in 1852 married at Wareham. They moved to the tiny hamlet of Birdsmoorgate between Beaminster and Axbridge, where Martha opened a grocery store and John worked as a wagoner. The nature of his business kept him away for long hours, possibly days at a time. Often when he returned home he was drunk and would sleep on the cottage floor.

Another lady in the hamlet was Mary Davies, the butcher's wife. She took in washing, running a small laundry business. She was closer to John's age and quite attractive. Rumours began to circulate that John Brown was perhaps having an affair with her. Martha became increasingly suspicious.

The fateful day

The 5th of July, 1856, turned out to be the tragic day on which John Brown would lose his life. He and a fellow wagoner shared a breakfast, which Martha had prepared, loaded their wagons with timber and set off for Beaminster. They'd not gone far when they gave a lift to Mary Davies who got off a bit further on to see to her laundry. They arrived at Beaminster at lunch time, delivered their load and headed towards home. Around mid-afternoon, and about halfway home, they stopped at a pub and stayed there until late into the evening. Meanwhile, an irate Martha heard the news that her John had been seen giving a lift to Mary Davies.

It was the early hours of the morning before he arrived home, much the worse for drink. Martha had supper waiting for him. By daybreak the following morning, he was dead. Martha ran to get help, explaining that he had been kicked in the head by the horse some way from the house and had only just managed to make his way home. But there was no blood on the horse's hooves, nor on the road, and the head wounds were more akin to those caused by an axe.

Dorset's last female hanged in public

Seventeen days later, Martha appeared at the Dorchester Quarter Sessions charged with murder. Evidence was presented showing that John had taken a horse whip to her. Her former employer testified as to her normally mild and gentle nature, but the evidence against her was overwhelming. She was convicted and condemned to death by hanging. When she walked out to the gallows, in what is now the North Square prison car park, a crowd of some 3,000 were waiting to view the spectacle. She was still an attractive woman and her hair had been groomed to perfection. So overcome was the prison chaplain that he could not perform his duty and it was the Rev. Moule who walked with her on her final journey.

At the base of the scaffold, she shook hands with the gathered officials and began to ascend the 39 steps. Part way up, she stopped as Calcraft, the executioner, manacled her hands. At the top of the steps, he placed the white hood over her head and slipped the noose around her neck. He then descended the steps to take up his position beneath the trap door where he would pull away the bolt which held it in place. There was then an embarrassing delay as it was pointed out that he had not strapped her legs together. It was now raining heavily and her moistened clothes clung to her body.

With Calcraft back in position, the crowd were completely silent as they awaited the end. Calcraft pulled away the bolt. Amongst the waiting crowd was the young Thomas Hardy observing 'what a fine figure she showed against the sky as she hung in the misty rain, and how the tight black silk gown set off her shape as she wheeled half-round and back', words he would pen some 70 years later, and words that tell us that death was not instantaneous. The rotating was her body's desperate attempts to struggle for air as she suffocated. Her body hung for the regulation one hour before being taken down.

James Seale

Stoke Abbott is a pretty little village just south of Beaminster. It was here in 1858 that John Hutchings owned a pair of cottages in Anchor Lane. He lived in one of these and collected rent from the occupants of the other. They were Rebecca Guppy and her 23-year-old daughter Sarah Ann. They shared the cottage with labourer James Seale, the 19-year-old son of Job and Hannah Seale. They were all born and bred residents of Stoke Abbott.

Stoke Abbott in the 19th century.

Sarah suffered from a minor deformity but was attractive nonetheless, with a quick and intelligent sense of humour.

On 30th April, 1858, neighbours noticed that the cottage shared by Seale and the Guppy ladies was on fire. The villagers soon extinguished the blaze but were then shocked to find Sarah's body on the kitchen floor. Her throat had been cut with a cheese knife. Her hands, arms and breast showed other injuries suggesting that she had struggled to defend her honour. At the time of the crime, all the other villagers except James Seale had been at work. Seale already had a criminal record, having served four months for robbery. He was the only suspect and was subsequently arrested and found guilty. Some fifteen weeks later, on 10th August, he was taken to the gallows at Dorchester prison, dressed in a white coarse cotton garment, and hanged. William Calcraft was once again in charge of proceedings. This was Dorset's last public execution.

High on the hills, three miles distant, Thomas Hardy had just watched his second and 'never again' public hanging.

Haunted Highways

Travelling through rural Dorset is always a pleasure but at one time it was a risky business. The roads were frequented by highwaymen and smugglers, of which there were plenty, especially along the Dorset coast. Although they are long gone, it seems their spirits remain and have a habit of popping up quite unexpectedly.

Bus and train journeys

Back in the 1970s, my good friends, David and Hilary Fry, were travelling by bus on the A354 just outside Winterborne Whitechurch. As they approached the village, they both saw what appeared to be a Cavalier. He was standing in the road in such a way that the bus driver was obliged to stop. Leaving his cab, he approached the man who promptly moved across the road, fading away through a solid hedge as if it wasn't there. The bus driver went looking for the man but to no avail. There was only the thick, solid hedge through which he had disappeared. Perhaps the hedge wasn't there in the days when the Cavalier originally made that journey. His attire suggested that he belonged to the 17th century. The bemused driver, unsettled by the experience, and needing to know that he wasn't hallucinating, asked his passengers if they could describe what they had just seen, if indeed they had seen anything. Without exception, all present described exactly the same experience.

Sightings such as these beg the question 'Do ghosts really exist?' The sceptic's opinion will be that such sightings are all in the imagination. But how can so many people, all sharing the same visual experience, all be imagining the same images at exactly the same time? More recently, in 1991, there was the case of two train drivers claiming that they had hit a figure as they were passing through the Bincombe tunnel, to the north of Upwey station. They stopped the train to find the victim but found nothing. The police investigation which followed, likewise revealed no presence. Here was yet another example of more than one witness to the same ghostly event.

That same year, near Wareham, a security worker had the most implausible experience. As he was doing his rounds in his van, he saw a similar van coming towards him. In fact it was so similar that he paid closer attention and soon realised that not only was the registration the same, but it was himself driving the other van, albeit in the opposite direction! It was like a mirror image without a mirror.

Coach and Horses

Most of us are sceptics at heart and will instinctively doubt most ghost stories. Even more dubious are those tales in which it is claimed that only members of the resident family can see the ghosts concerned. Such is the example with the phantom coach and horses of Woolbridge Manor, near Wool, which is claimed to be visible only to those with Turberville blood in their veins. A similar story relates to its near neighbour, Hethfelton House, but this time it is claimed that only those with some connection to the house itself will experience the apparition of the coach and horses heading off towards the River Frome.

Stepping back in time to the days of coach travel brings us to a number of sightings. A coach and horses driven by a headless coachman travels along Coach Lane, West Lulworth; and at Trent Manor near Sherborne, the sound of galloping hooves will be heard as they travel along the old road, allegedly belonging to a coach and horses which mysteriously disappeared. On the road from Beaminster to Stoke Abbott there are sightings of a coach and four horses, driven by a wicked landowner who is doomed to relentlessly travel this road by way of punishment for his cruel behaviour.

Wolfeton House

But these are all coach and horse stories from the open highway, where perhaps they belong. Far more unusual is the phantom horse and coach which appears on the staircase of 16th-century Wolfeton House. For many centuries this was the ancestral home of the Trenchard family and lies in the water meadows by the rivers Cerne and Frome. Tragic circumstances surrounded the life of its one-time owner, the 17th-century Sir Thomas Trenchard. Rarely is someone's ghost seen during their own lifetime, but that was the case when Sir Thomas saw the premonition of his wife, with blood gushing from her slit throat. Unbeknown to Sir Thomas at the time, this vision foretold the event which was to take place just a matter of hours later, when his wife took her own life in the very way the vision predicted.

But this has strayed away from the theme of coach and horses and from the bizarre event which is repeated even today in ghostly form. Sir Thomas was nothing if not extrovert and on one occasion, having boasted of his abilities with horse and carriage, he agreed to a sizeable wager that he could drive a carriage and horse up the staircase of his mansion. He won the wager and as if to prove that it really happened, it keeps on reappearing!

Another reported haunting from the same house is the sound of the footsteps of Cornelius, an Irish Catholic monk who for some unknown reason was hanged, drawn and quartered at Dorchester.

Road kill

Why spirits should wander the countryside in ghostly form is a great unanswered question, but one certainty is that many of these lost souls are the result of tragic deaths whilst travelling. On Newton Heath near Studland, a ghostly white donkey haunts the area, its master having been robbed and murdered as he made his way home for Christmas. In Millhams Lane on the northern edge of Bournemouth, the pale ghost of a lady has been seen trying to tempt people off the bridge at the site where she was run down and killed by a horse and carriage.

A half mile east of Trent near Sherborne is the deep pit known as Trent Barrow, often described as bottomless, such is the depth of the water. Legend tells how in the darkness of night, a coach with its horses and all of its passengers failed to see the pool and plunged into the depths. No one was spared and not a trace was left of their former presence. Now on nights which are equally dark and stormy, the screaming voices of the passengers and the sound of galloping horses will be heard to remind us of their fate.

The oldest ghost of them all

Arguably the oldest of Dorset's ghosts, and perhaps the oldest in the country, is that of the Bronze Age warrior who haunts Cranborne Chase and has been recorded at various times since the 1920s. He appears dressed in furs and mounted bareback on a stocky and rugged-looking horse, almost certainly an Exmoor pony. In his hand he carries a Bronze Age axe suggesting that here was once a warrior who still defends his territory as he gallops across the chase. As if to confirm the theory, a modern-day excavation of a nearby barrow revealed the skeletal remains of a man and his horse.

THE ARCHITECT, THE PIANIST AND THE CHAUFFEUR

Bournemouth hit the national headlines in 1935 when the internationally-acclaimed architect Francis Rattenbury was murdered, the result of a love triangle involving his much younger, glamorous wife and their chauffeur. But the story begins many years before.

Francis Mawson Rattenbury was born and raised in Leeds, Yorkshire. Having completed his training to become an architect,

Parliament Buildings, Victoria, designed by Francis Rattenbury.

he decided that it was not in England that he would find his fortune, but somewhere in the New World. An opportunity arose for him to travel to Canada, doing work for the government on a number of major projects. The potential for fame and fortune beckoned and he heeded the call. His journey in 1891 took him to Vancouver in British Columbia, on the western seaboard of Canada. Before his first year in the province was complete, he had won a coveted prize, in a competition open to all architects, to design the Parliament Buildings for Victoria. The rapidly growing city had been chosen to become the administrative capital for the province of British Columbia and needed a building befitting its ambitions. Francis Rattenbury's achievement was an outstanding success.

Early success, early fame

The finished building was magnificent and gained widespread acclaim. Rattenbury's name was soon on the tongues of those seeking architects with ability and vision. He shot to fame and his services were in great demand. Further successes followed: railway hotels, the magnificent and luxurious Empress Hotel which took pride of place on the city's seafront, and Vancouver's Law Courts.

In 1898 he married Florence Nunn and they had two children, Frank and Mary. At the tail end of 1923, now aged 56, his life was to change completely. Perhaps it was a mid-life crisis. He had just won a major contract for another major building project and was celebrating his success at the Empress Hotel. Also there was a 27-year-old professional pianist who performed under the name of Lozanne. She was charming and quite beautiful. She was also unattached, having tragically lost one husband and carelessly lost the other.

Her real name was Alma Pakenham. She had grown up in British Columbia and her adolescent years spent in Vancouver, where her mother encouraged her to learn the pianoforte. It was an investment which paid off and Alma became a musician of professional standard. She was 19 years old when she married her sweetheart, Caledon Dolling, from Northern Ireland. With the outbreak of the First World War, Caledon enlisted into the British Army and Alma followed him to England.

Alma's life then took a tragic turn. Her husband had been posted to the Front and, in common with so many wives and mothers back at home, the little brown envelope was delivered by

Francis Rattenbury

Alma Packenham

the telegram boy, bearing the news that Caledon had been killed at the Battle of the Somme. She was devastated at the loss of her childhood sweetheart, finding it difficult to face the future without him. But Alma's courage and fortitude shone through and she took the decision that it was time to take her part in the war effort. She decided to join an ambulance unit, not just any unit, but a Scottish one which she knew would be serving behind the French lines. In the battlefield arena, she demonstrated such bravery that she was awarded the French Croix de Guerre, with star and palm.

The war came to an end and with it a time for reflection, a time to look forward to a new era. Alma had by now met Captain Compton Pakenham. They married and moved to America where their son Christopher was born. Sadly, the marriage was not to last and Alma left her husband, taking their son to live with her mother back in Vancouver where she returned to her career as a pianist. Meanwhile, she was named as the guilty party in her divorce case and was free and single once more.

It was after one of her performances in Victoria that she finished the evening at the Empress Hotel, sharing a seasonal drink with one of her friends. It was that party time of the year, just two days before New Year's Eve 1923; the very sort of environment and atmosphere where new friends are acquired and romances blossom between the most unlikely characters. It was the same evening that Francis Rattenbury was celebrating his newly-won contract. The two met for the first time, she the young, glamorous and talented divorcee, he twice her age but apparently influential and affluent. The affair began and was soon public knowledge.

Divorce

Rattenbury's wife cited Alma Pakenham in the divorce case (the second time she had earned the honour!) and the two sons from the marriage stayed with her. Unlike modern times, in those days divorce was considered a disgrace and would destroy a reputation. Alma's fame as a pianist and her awards for front-line bravery were no protection from the scandal. Rattenbury's reputation as a leading architect and pillar of local society was also no protection against the social humiliation he was about to suffer, even his friends now turning their backs on him. The breakdown of the marriage itself proved to be a bitter and spiteful period for all concerned. Rattenbury even had the heating and lighting turned off in the family home, where his wife and children still lived, and openly flaunted his affair. It became impossible for the two to remain in Victoria.

Manor Road, Bournemouth

They married and moved, along with Alma's son Christopher, to live in Dorset, choosing 5 Manor Road in the East Cliff area of Bournemouth, a house known as Villa Madeira. It was here that their already scandalous lives were to create an even greater scandal. Their son John was born in 1929 and all appeared well with the marriage. However, this was far from the truth. Sex between the couple was non-existent from the time of John's birth. Alma slept upstairs in the marital bed; Francis slept downstairs with a nightly bottle of whisky.

Alma, with son Christopher and now John, had the benefit of a live-in housekeeper, Irene Riggs, who was also a companion to Alma. But Alma needed more than female companionship. Still in her thirties and still very attractive, she was missing the creature comforts. In September 1934, an advertisement was placed in the

Bournemouth Daily Echo seeking a willing lad of 14 to 18-years-old, preferably Scout-trained, to carry out housework. Eighteen-year-old George Percy Stoner answered the advert and was duly appointed as a chauffeur and handyman.

George was a quiet lad, shy and retiring in nature. His childhood years had been spent partly with his parents and partly with his grandparents, all of whom lived in Bournemouth. Although Alma had advertised for a 14 to 18-year-old, George was at the top end of the range, strongly-built and handsome, but illiterate and innocent in affairs of the heart. Within the first two months, he had been seduced into a passionate affair with Alma, and one which was blatantly open. Alma bought him clothes and took him with her to a hotel in London. In fairness to George, we have to assume that the 18-year-old inexperienced lad had fallen for the mature woman's advances, and she was, after all, his employer. Alma's otherwise dreary domestic life had finally found an adventurous outlet.

With the open nature of the affair, Francis Rattenbury became increasingly depressed and by the end of 1934 was suicidal. George Stoner was, by now, sleeping nightly in Alma's bed. His affections for Alma grew ever stronger and he became obsessive and possessive. When Alma and Francis spent time together, perhaps going to London, Stoner's jealousy festered. Perhaps this was what Alma wanted. Perhaps she was manipulating her young lover towards the disposal of her husband in the same way that she had manipulated Stoner into her bed.

After one such trip to London, when Francis was in a deep depression, Alma suggested a visit to friends in Bridport. Before the trip could take place, Stoner visited his parents to borrow a wooden mallet, allegedly to put up a garden screen. By the end of that same day, Francis Rattenbury was lying with his head caked in blood, and his doctor was arranging for him to be taken to hospital. When the blood was cleaned away from the matted hair, it became obvious that his head had been battered. The police were notified and their investigation began.

Murder

By the time the police arrived at the Rattenbury home, in the early hours of the morning, Alma was almost incoherent, either drunk or drugged. All they could really make out was that she had 'done him in', which she repeatedly confessed. In the cold light of the following morning, she continued her confession and was arrested for attempted murder. The days passed and back at Manor Road, Stoner also confessed, in confidence, to Irene Riggs, the housekeeper that it was actually he who had committed the crime. Irene notified the police, perhaps to protect her employer, and Stoner was also taken into custody. The following day, Francis Rattenbury died and the charges were upgraded to murder.

The case attracted massive national interest, so much so that the court at Winchester was inadequate and the trial began at the Old Bailey on 27th May, 1935. Both Alma and George Stoner stood accused, both having been persuaded to plead not guilty. Throughout the trial, Stoner maintained complete silence other than to confirm his name. In contrast, Alma made a strong and robust defence on her own behalf.

Was Stoner guilty or was he protecting the woman he loved? Was Alma the real killer, and in a cold-blooded act of betrayal, ready to watch as Stoner went down? Herein lies the mystery. For the jury, there was no doubt. Stoner was found guilty of murder and sentenced to death. Alma was given her freedom.

Suicide

The case had been much publicised. Here was a young 18-year-old lad, the victim of a cold, manipulative woman, more than twenty years his senior. When Alma left the court, descending the steps of the Old Bailey, she was greeted by a booing crowd, venting their disgust and disbelief. After a few days spent in the capital, she took a train back to Christchurch where she walked across the fields to the Three Arches railway bridge. There she wrote notes for those she left behind, walked towards the water's edge and stabbed herself six times in the chest until finally she fell forward into the river, mortally wounded and dead within seconds.

The frustrated pianist and songwriter, during her days in a prison cell awaiting her trial, had written a song which was later published under the title *Mrs Rattenbury's Prison Song*. The lyrics of the song and the notes she had written provided proof of her real love for the condemned Stoner. Believing that his execution was imminent, her suicide was an act of shame. She was buried at Wimborne Road cemetery, a matter of yards from her husband, their final resting places ironically close but yet apart. At her interment, signatures were already being collected to plead for clemency for George Stoner. Such was the national feeling, that by the time the petition had been presented, it contained almost a third of a million signatures. Amongst those who presented it to the Home Secretary were Bournemouth's MP and mayor. The petition mercifully proved successful and the death sentence was commuted to a life sentence.

The quiet man that was George Stoner proved to be a model prisoner and, thanks to the need for recruits into the army, he earned his release after serving just seven years. George had been granted the opportunity to rebuild his life and in 1942 enlisted into the army to serve his country during what was left of the Second World War. He was one of the many who took part in the D-Day landings. After the war, he returned to his former home in Redhill, Bournemouth, from where he was able to embark on a new life. He married, raised a family and lived out the rest of his life in Ensbury Park in Bournemouth. In 2000, he died in Christchurch hospital, aged 83. In a strange quirk of fate, it was exactly 65 years since the death of Francis Rattenbury.

Alma's two sons were also able to rebuild their lives, both embarking on professional careers; with John Rattenbury following in his father's footsteps as a successful architect in the USA.

But who really killed Francis? Was it his wife? Had Stoner carried the blame in an act of love? Or was it he who was the killer, despite Alma's repeated confessions? Would he have been foolish enough to use the wooden mallet which he had only borrowed from his grandparents earlier that day? No one will know the answer for certain. Those who knew took their secret to the grave.

THEY SHARED THE SAME GALLOWS

The nine o'clock threshold is a recent innovation in television broadcasting, there to protect those of a sensitive disposition from scenes of a distasteful nature. We are so well protected from the raw and unseemly side of life, that it is difficult now to understand how public executions could ever have been so popular. But such was the case and the general public turned out in their thousands to watch these spectacles. So a double hanging was an opportunity not to be missed. Such was the case on 27th March 1863, when Edwin Preedy and Charles Fooks were simultaneously dispatched to meet their maker.

Edwin Alfred Preedy

It's a personal view but too often, especially in the case of violent youngsters, there is an attitude which says the offender is not to blame. *'He had a difficult childhood; what more could we expect? He's not to blame – society is to blame.'* Generally speaking, I do not share that attitude. We are all masters of our own destiny. We make choices along the way and have to live with those decisions.

Admittedly, some are born with a silver spoon and others are not, but we should all accept responsibility for our own actions. However, once in a blue moon, I can honestly say that it really is the treatment someone receives in their childhood that accounts for their actions in later life. Edwin Preedy was just such a case.

He was born in Leamington Spa, Warwickshire, in 1842. There was no father figure in the family. When he was four years old, his younger brother Joseph was born. It was at this time that he took a nasty fall down a staircase in their home, cracking his head as he landed. He bled profusely from nose and mouth. This greatly concerned his mother, Ann, and his aunt who had seen what had happened but Ann earned a meagre wage as a shirt-maker and couldn't afford a doctor; hence Edwin received no proper medical attention. From that day on, he became a very troubled child. Neurotic and requiring constant attention, at night he could only sleep if he slept with his mother. His mother soon moved to London and it was there that fortune cast a dark spell over young Edwin. Matters worsened when his mother met and married Bill Edwards.

Edwards was a printer, a violent man with a quick temper and no tolerance to ill-mannered or strangely-behaved children, as was the case with Edwin. Edwin was by now attending school and there, because he was so different from the other children, he was bullied relentlessly. Arriving home, there was little comfort to be found. His stepfather said the boy should toughen up. He couldn't keep sleeping with his mother. His night-time screams of terror were met with a beating from his stepfather and his mother was too afraid to intervene. When his aunt witnessed the bruising, she challenged the mother to stand up for her son, but soon realised that both mother and child would take a beating if they dared to challenge Edwards. There appeared to be no hope for the young lad.

On the streets

Aged just thirteen, Edwin took to the streets, possibly kicked out by his stepfather. Living the life of a street urchin, and a deranged one at that, he was eventually taken to the St Giles workhouse in London's West End. The matron of the workhouse took one look at him and declared the lad should be in the asylum, not the workhouse. He was kicking and growling, thrashing around and foaming at the mouth like a rabid dog. A medical examination determined that he was insane but probably only temporarily, as the result of a fever. For days on end, he was tied down, his restraints only being slackened at meal times. Thick with lice and other infestations, he was stripped, washed and had his head shaved. It was then that the full extent of his injuries and scarring, testament to the cruelty that he had suffered, became apparent.

After weeks of decent care and attention, he calmed down, smartened up and was deemed fit to return home to the care of his mother. Old enough to work, he became a printer's apprentice to his stepfather, but it wasn't long before the brutality recommenced. He couldn't respond to discipline or orders. Speak to him pleasantly and he was fine; anything less than that was lighting the blue touch paper. Before long he left and made his way back to Warwickshire, but he could only survive by stealing and consequently spent eight months confined in Warwick Castle.

Despite his hatred of discipline, on his release from prison, he joined the army, was promoted to corporal and then deserted. Life on the run was short-lived and he was soon back in prison in Carmarthen for a ten-week stretch. Arrested initially for a criminal rather than military act, the prison governor soon discovered that the army was still looking for their missing deserter. Preedy, up until now, had been relatively calm, but when the warder announced that the army wanted him back, Preedy went berserk, behaving once again like a wild animal, attacking the two warders who escorted him back to his cell. He threw the desk onto the governor, cracked open the head of one of the guards, and then used a chair to attack the other guards who were coming to the rescue.

Transfer to Dorset

When the army collected what belonged to them, Preedy was securely shackled in heavy irons. Only too keen to see the back of him, the army gave him a dishonourable discharge and let him loose in west Wales. Once again he had to steal to keep body and soul together, gaining himself another three-year stretch in prison. But the Welsh prisons were unable to deal with his increasingly violent behaviour and he was sent to the harsher Millbank prison in London. His refusal to work brought a reprimand from the governor and on his way back to his cell, frustrated and angry once again at his treatment, he went berserk, attacking and severely beating his escort as he snarled and roared like an animal. This earned him a flogging. The governor soon realised that this prisoner was far too dangerous for his establishment and this is where Dorset enters the story. Preedy was transferred to the notoriously tough Portland prison.

By now, September 1862, Preedy had developed a pathological hatred for prison guards and had boasted to a fellow prisoner as to how he would kill one of the guards and he was prepared to 'swing' for his crime. His wish was to be granted. Three prisoners, with a guard, were approaching his cell. It was a routine visit to collect the cutlery used to eat his meal. They passed from cell to cell, collecting in all of the utensils. When they got to Preedy's cell, he stood away from the door, standing to attention, as was the requirement. When one of the prisoners stepped inside the cell, Preedy held out his arm to pass the knife, fork and spoon to the fellow prisoner, dropping the fork and spoon as he did so, but hanging onto the knife. When the fellow prisoner stooped to pick up the dropped items, Preedy leapt past him, launched himself at the guard, grabbing him around the neck with one arm whilst he stabbed deep into his throat using the other.

Murder

Two of the prisoners wrestled Preedy to the ground as cries of 'Murder!' echoed around the prison cells. Charles Evans, perhaps the most popular warder, staggered momentarily and fell dead. A second warder arrived as the two convicts continued to wrestle with Preedy. Drawing his cutlass, the warder swiped Preedy with the flat of the blade, knocking him unconscious. When he came to, he was asked why he had killed Evans. He said he had a grievance, as simple as that.

A visit from the prison chaplain was not well received. Preedy threw another animal-like tantrum and the chaplain was whisked away for his own safety, with Preedy declaring he would only communicate with a Catholic priest, albeit he wasn't a Catholic, but this was typical of his unpredictable behaviour.

The following morning, he was transferred to Dorchester prison, charged with murder. On his way, he told the police inspector who was with him that he wasn't really a Catholic and that he didn't hold a grudge against the warder he had murdered; he just happened to be the first warder to come along after he had decided to kill one. Throughout the trip, Preedy was calm and quiet, deceptively so. On being faced with solitary confinement, once again he went berserk.

By now it was realised that it was after periods of isolation that Preedy became violent, but it was too risky to lock him up with other prisoners. Locked in his cell, he tore his clothes to shreds and was left naked for days at a time. A month of violent behaviour did not bode well for the trial, but then something happened that changed him. He took into his care an injured sparrow and calmed down to become a quiet and caring individual. Other injured birds were brought to him and he became the perfect prisoner.

The trial

The day of his trial arrived and it was a smartly-dressed Preedy who calmly entered the dock. The trial began and all seemed well-ordered until one of his previous fellow prisoners began to give his evidence. Preedy reverted to form, cursed the witness and tried to leap over the dock to get to him. Six battered and bruised officers finally pinned him down. The judge enquired as to whether or not the prisoner was fit to proceed. He asked Preedy if he needed a few minutes to compose himself. In reply, Preedy asked the judge if they had met before and then claimed that the judge had somehow altered, as if he was hallucinating. Despite this, the judge declared he was clearly sane and that, in the interest of safety and of getting on with the trial, Preedy should be restrained. His legs were strapped together and his arms strapped to his body. Again Preedy went berserk and in a fit of violence, snapped every piece of restraining leather work. The judge ran from the court, not returning until Preedy had been clapped in irons. Shackled hand and foot, he thrashed and raved until collapsing from exhaustion. A few minutes later, he kicked off again, this time bringing proceedings to a complete halt whilst the judge once more consulted his learned colleagues. Was the prisoner insane?

His mother was one of those who gave evidence during this unusual and chaotic trial, explaining the fall he had as a child and how he had been ill-treated. But there could be no mitigation. He was found guilty and sentenced to death by hanging. The judge advised him strongly that he should seek spiritual guidance in an attempt to make peace with his maker. Surprisingly perhaps, Preedy did just that. During his final days, he was mentored by the Reverend Henry Moule, the vicar of Fordington near Dorchester. He brought great comfort to the prisoner, spending countless hours with him in his final days. On 27th March 1863, after taking his last confession and showing great fortitude, he took the final steps which led to the gallows.

Charles Fooks

'I didn't like my cousin. He looked at me in a funny way.' That was the reason Charles Fooks gave as justification for committing murder. Charles Fooks had a troubled mind in a troubled body. By modern standards, he was clearly insane – but that was not the opinion of Judge Shee when he was taken to his trial.

Fooks was a farmer at Walditch, just to the east of Bridport. He employed two men and two boys but was not a popular employer. He was a man prone to violent and unpredictable tempers. His cousin Daniel Stone lived as a close neighbour and did his best to keep a friendly relationship with Fooks but was fighting a losing battle. Some believed that Fooks fell out with Stone when Stone objected to Fooks's marriage proposal to his sister. Fooks denied this and became obsessed with the idea that Daniel Stone was continually standing outside his house, listening to any conversations within.

His behaviour became increasingly paranoid and on several occasions he told friends and neighbours that he would shoot Daniel Stone. He was something of a gun fanatic, having several in his home. Friends and relations, even his doctor, visited him to try and persuade him not to do anything foolish. Most of them met with a violent reaction and left in fear for their own lives. Each time he received a visitor, Fooks would complain of the pain he was in, physically and mentally. Evidence of his instability had been present when, years before, he had sealed all the doors and windows of his house. It appeared to be an attempt to keep evil out but inside he was slowly suffocating.

Despite his paranoid behaviour, his relatives did their best to help, including his niece Martha Hallett who was living in with him. She was there one evening when a solicitor's clerk, Daniel Read called at the house. When the dogs barked, Fooks was convinced that his cousin Daniel Stone was outside. Fooks's temper was fired up and out he went with a loaded gun, pledging to shoot Stone like a rook. On a later occasion, he rushed into the street and fired a shot at an unseen stranger, fortunately without harming anyone. Then he became convinced that his two young farm hands, who were decent, hard-working lads, were continually mocking him. He sacked them, an action he later confessed to regretting, stating that his temper had got the better of him.

Some days later, Daniel Stone was walking along a lane with another resident when Fooks popped up from behind a hedge and hurled a boulder which knocked Stone to the ground. 'I didn't mean to do that' declared Fooks as he turned to walk away. When Martha Hallett heard about it, she was so concerned that, the following morning, she packed her bags and returned home to the safety of her family. She told of her fear of living with such a deranged man. As a compromise, her stepfather returned with her and the pair stayed with Fooks for a few days during which Fooks told the stepfather how he was troubled with pains in his stomach and head. Convinced that Fooks was sane and safe, the stepfather returned home, leaving Martha to care for Fooks. It didn't last long.

A few evenings later, Fooks had another violent turn, accusing Martha of mocking him behind his back. She was terrified of what he might do. The following morning, she was on her way back home, and this time for good. Half an hour later, the inevitable happened. Daniel Stone was walking past Fooks's house when Fooks stepped out with his gun and shot him. Villagers who saw what happened, rushed to Stone's side. Two men picked him up and carried him to his father's house where he died.

Meanwhile, a second shot was heard coming from Fooks's house. Those brave enough to enter, found Fooks with blood coming from his head, but he was still alive. The second shot had fired the wad from the barrel through the ceiling, but it contained no pellets. That was the series of events which led to his trail where Judge Shee received the guilty verdict from the jury. Placing the black cap on his head, he announced the death penalty.

A shared scaffold

Seven o'clock on the morning of their execution, 27th March 1863, 20-year-old Edwin Preedy and 49-year-old Charles Fooks were led out onto the flat-top roof of Dorchester prison. They were on their way to providing the entertainment awaited by the crowd of over 5,000 spectators, mostly women. Multiple executions were rare, once or twice in a lifetime. The prison governor had received the news from the Secretary of State that there was nothing to justify the commutation of their sentences.

The gallows had been erected over the north gate of the prison. Fooks, sullen at first, began to express his sorrow for what he had done and prayed with the chaplain and schoolmaster who were there to comfort him in his final moments. But it was Preedy that held the gaze of the spectators. His reputation for unexpected violent behaviour augured well for a spectacular finish but he held himself proud and was completely in control. With the aid of the Reverend Moule, who accompanied him to the scaffold, he had already drawn up a long and contrite address. At the scaffold, he apologised to the officers present for his violent behaviour, offering to shake their hands but no one accepted the offer, except William Calcraft, the executioner.

Their heads were covered, each with a black hood, and the nooses placed around their necks as they stood on the platform's trap door. Calcraft pulled away the bolt and the condemned men dropped to their deaths. Fooks, a heavy man at 6 ft 2 ins, died instantly. Preedy, short in stature and slim in build, took a little longer, death coming only after a few twitches. An hour after their execution, their bodies were taken down and the crowd drifted away to their homes.

The Reverend Moule, not one to miss a financial opportunity, published his recollections of Preedy's final days in a best-selling publication *Hope against Hope.*

From Beyond the Grave

There can be no doubt that there have been, and will continue to be, occasions when justice is not done. In the case of violent crimes, this is especially true. In times past, when the death penalty was the ultimate punishment, the perpetrators of such deeds would do all in their power to disguise the crime. So wouldn't it be nice, wouldn't it be justice, if the deceased victim could put things right from beyond the grave? There are at least two examples in Dorset where that certainly appears to have happened.

John Daniel of Beaminster

It was 1728 and John Daniel was a schoolboy who had been attending St Mary's church for his schooling. It was believed that John had died from a fit and he was buried with no suspicions around the circumstances of his death. Alas, he had been murdered but no one knew, other than his killer who was unlikely to confess. It was down to the recently departed John to make sure that the deed was discovered.

Several weeks after John's death, he was to appear in an apparition to no fewer than five fellow pupils, albeit one of these had never met him. The school classroom was the gallery within the church, which had its own unique entrance. After Saturday classes, one of the pupils would deliver the keys to the parish clerk. It was on Saturday, 27th June 1728, when twelve of the boys, class having been dismissed by its master, stayed to play ball in the churchyard. It was around midday, and hence broad daylight. Four boys went back into the school to get some old pens but soon left when they heard what they described as a brass pan being struck.

Back with the rest of the lads, they described their experience. Convinced that someone was playing a prank on them, and full of bravado, all twelve boys went to investigate. Nothing happened and no one was to be found. They turned round to head back to their game when a second noise was heard. In panic, they were running around the church when, on reaching the west door, they could hear the sound of hymns and a sermon being delivered, albeit the noises were brief and faded away almost as soon as they were heard.

Somewhat bemused, but not particularly bothered, they continued to play until one lad went back into the church to collect his book and returned to the group declaring he had seen a coffin lying on one of the school benches. There was no doubt as to what he saw – he was within six feet of it!

All the lads rushed to the classroom door to see if his story was true. For five of them, it was. All five, but only those five, could see the coffin, possibly because they were the ones at the front and the others never got a look in. These five lads not only saw the coffin, but also the ghostly apparition of their old classmate John Daniels, sitting close to his coffin. The first lad to recognise him was John's half-brother who declared that there was his brother wearing a coat exactly like his own. The two always dressed alike. His ghostly brother held a pen in one hand and had a book placed before him as if to start writing. So shocked was the brother that, despite attempts to stop him, he threw a stone at his brother's ghost and it disappeared.

With so many witnesses, the local magistrate, Colonel Broadrepp, decided he had to take the matter seriously and he interviewed each lad in turn. Aged from nine to twelve, one by one they described what they had seen. Each described the apparition, even down to the very detail of the hinges on the coffin. Now it has to be stressed that one of these witnesses had never met or even seen John Daniel and yet he was able, as one of the oldest in the group, to give a very precise description, including the presence of a white cloth around the hand of the ghost.

Daniel's body had been found in a field a couple of hundred yards from his home. Because his mother told how he apparently suffered from fits, he was buried without the benefit of an inquest. The lady, who had laid out his body, explained how Daniel had injured his hand and it had been bound up with a white cloth for a good four days. She removed this when she laid him out.

The magistrate felt there was sufficient cause to have Daniel's body disinterred so that a proper coroner's inquest could be held. The coroner's verdict was that Daniel had been strangled. Two reliable ladies told the inquest that they had seen the body two days after its discovery and there were black bruises around the neck. The coffin maker confirmed what he had seen. Although we know that Daniel's demise had been the result of a murder, there is no evidence to suggest that anyone was ever brought to justice. Perhaps that is why it is claimed that the tearful face of his ghost can still be seen outside the church.

In August 1998, the *Bridport News* reported a follow-up to this tale. David Potter was out one morning at Bell Farm. It was a quarter to five and, despite the early hour, he was out and about in one of his fields which was next to the site where John Daniels was buried. His cows were in calf and he was keeping a close eye on them. Although it was still dark, he was approaching one of his cows without using his torch. In the faint light available, he could see two figures in the field, standing over a cow and staring down at it. Were they in fact staring at the site of Daniel's murder? Or the site where his body was found? Was this Daniel and his mother? One was a woman with a long, white, flowing robe. The other was a young child dressed in dark clothing, his face turned away from the farmer's view. They were no more than a few yards away from the farmer and did not appear to be ghosts, but solid figures.

A cold chill hit the farmer who shone his torch directly at the couple. The woman's eyes shone bright pink. Whilst he froze to the spot, the couple turned and walked away. A cow lying in their path got up and moved aside. Shortly after, came the sound of the gate to the graveyard closing. The farmer was well aware that this event came after he had recently been asked by a living relative of John Daniels if he could indicate the location of John Daniel's grave.

Neville Heath – Serial Killer

It was an early morning stroll for a lady with her dog along Branksome Chine, a suburb of Poole. The high banks of rhododendrons were in full blossom and provided corridors of privacy where villains could lie in wait, or where a body could wait to be discovered. To her horror, and having had her attention attracted by the droning hum of a swarm of flies, her daily routine was shattered by the discovery of a mutilated and almost completely naked body. It was the remains of Bournemouth's lost lady, Doreen Marshall. It was a discovery which solved more than one mystery. It was also the remains of Neville Heath's final victim.

Neville Heath.

National Service and criminal activities

Neville George Clevely Heath was born at Ilford, Essex, in June 1917. His father was a barber and must have put himself under considerable financial pressure to ensure his son received the best education his income could afford by sending him to a private school. In 1934 Neville joined the army in the Rifle Battalion and stayed with them for two years, presumably seeing out his national service. In 1936, Heath joined the Royal Air Force, but was dismissed after being court-martialled in September 1937 when he went absent without leave. Perhaps the family support was no longer available to him because within a matter of weeks, he next appears on the radar when he is arrested for obtaining credit by fraud. He must have been a real character and cut quite a dash since he was able to convince those he defrauded that he was, at times, Lord Dudley and at other times Lieutenant-Colonel Armstrong.

A matter of months later, he was in trouble again, this time for forgery and housebreaking, stealing £50 of jewellery. In July 1938, his crimes resulted in a three-year sentence at Borstal, a prison institution for young offenders, where a regime of harsh discipline was used to 'build better characters'. Having served his time, he joined the Royal Army Service Corps as a private and must have created the right impression for by 1941 he's in the Middle East, having been granted a commission. But trouble was waiting just around the corner and he committed another fraud, went absent without leave and was court-martialled for a second time. He was being sent back to England when he escaped and headed for Johannesburg.

With a criminal record and a court-martial on his CV, he changed his name and under the alias of Armstrong, he joined the South African Air Force. Eventually the authorities discovered the true nature of his past history but his service had been so good, they decided to let matters lie. He was able to remain in their service and indeed he rose to the rank of Captain. In the middle of 1944, he was back in England, having been seconded to the RAF, and returned to South Africa in 1945 after the end of the Second World War. For a while, it looked as though he would finally settle down. He married and had a son. Before the end of December, 1946, he was court-martialled for his third and final time for wearing decorations to which he was not entitled. It seems a weak reason but perhaps, with the war over, it was time to move him on and he was sent back to England. His wife, perhaps now realising what a bad lot he was, left him.

The murders begin

His previous relatively petty crimes were soon to pale into insignificance. The following weeks were to witness some of the most horrific violence and sexually motivated crimes imaginable.

In May, 1946, Heath rented a room at the Pembridge Court Hotel in London's Notting Hill. Although he used his real name, he was not entitled to use the rank of Lieutenant-Colonel which is how he signed himself in. He also signed in his 'wife', Margery Gardner, whom he had met a matter of hours earlier. He was 29 years old and she was a 32-year-old actress who had deserted her husband and daughter to find fame in the city. Having spent an evening of heavy drinking together, they headed for the hotel where apparently, having stripped naked, she was tied up and whipped, and quite willingly spent the night with Heath.

The following month, on 15th June, Heath was in a dance hall in Chelsea. There he met the 19-year-old Yvonne Symonds and again introduced himself as Lieutenant-Colonel Neville Heath. She fell totally for his charm and stayed with him as they visited the Panama Club in Kensington and then the Overseas Club. The following day was spent in each other's company. By the end of the day, she had accepted his proposal of marriage and spent the night with him at the Pembridge Court Hotel. The commissioner was probably wondering by now which of the wives was actually the real one, if indeed either of them were! The following day, Yvonne returned to her parental home in Worthing, no doubt full of the joys of spring, itching to break the news to her parents.

Four days later, Heath was back at the Panama Club with Margery Gardner and the two of them, very drunk, went back to his hotel room at the Pembridge. Early the following morning, Heath caught the train to Worthing, to meet his new fiancée's family, leaving a murder scene in his wake.

Margery Gardner

The following day, the chambermaid at the Pembridge was unable to gain access to Heath's room and had to get the assistant manager to use the master key. There on the bed, face-up, lay the naked body of Margery Gardner. Her ankles were tied with a handkerchief. Her body had been mutilated; seventeen whip marks on her body, her nipples had been viciously bitten off and a short poker, which remained in the fireplace, inserted into her body and savagely rotated in what presumably had been a sexually perverted act, causing significant internal injuries. Her face was badly bruised. There was no sign of the whip but the pattern of the marks it had left showed a criss-cross diamond pattern as would be left if a riding crop had been used. It was only after all this torture had been inflicted on her, that she was finally suffocated.

The police were notified and clearly it was Heath, in whose room the body lay, who became the prime suspect. Later that day, the press were given some of the details of the murder and the name and description of Neville Heath.

Meanwhile, Heath had arrived at Worthing and booked into a hotel. Over lunch with his fiancée, he told her how there had apparently been a murder in his London hotel. They met again in the evening, sharing dinner when he expanded on his version of what had happened; how he'd seen the body. He claimed that he had let Margery use his room to entertain a friend, and that he, Heath, had spent the night somewhere else.

The following day, Heath received a phone call from Yvonne who told him how his name had appeared in the national daily newspapers, and that the police wanted to question him in connection with the murder. Heath needed to escape but he needed to send the police searching in the wrong direction. He wrote a note to the investigating officer, telling the same story he had told Yvonne, but this time saying that the name of the man Margery was to entertain was Jack somebody. He explained how he had returned to the room at about two in the morning, found the body, packed his gear and left for fear that he would be blamed.

Doreen Marshall

He quietly left Worthing, headed for Dorset and moved to Bournemouth where he checked into the Tollard Royal Hotel, under the name of Group Captain Rupert Brook. He had been there a week and a half when, on 3rd July 1946, he met Doreen Marshall, a 21-year-old who was staying at the Norfolk Hotel in Bournemouth, recovering from a severe bout of 'flu. She agreed to take afternoon tea with Heath and later met him at his hotel for dinner. At half past eleven, they left when he offered to walk her back to her hotel. That was the last time she was seen alive.

Two days later, the manager of the Norfolk Hotel notified the police that Doreen Marshall had not been seen for two days. The last time he saw her was when she asked for a taxi to take her to the Tollard Royal Hotel. The Norfolk Hotel manager rang his counterpart at the Tollard Royal, having heard that she had used the restaurant there the evening she had taken the taxi. As a result of that enquiry, the Tollard Royal manager asked Heath, alias Group Captain Rupert Brook as he knew him, if his dinner guest two nights before had been Doreen Marshall. Heath replied to the negative, claiming that his guest had been a lady of a different name whom he had known for many years.

At the manager's suggestion, Heath rang the local police and spoke to a detective who was handling the young lady's

Tollard Royal Hotel, Bournemouth.

disappearance. He agreed to go to the station to view a photo of the missing lady but, as he was viewing the photo, the observant detective was comparing Heath's features with a photo of Heath which had been issued by Scotland Yard. The detective raised the obvious question, 'Are you Neville Heath?'. Heath denied his true identity and another detective was sent to get Heath's jacket from his hotel. In the pocket were a pearl from Doreen Marshall's necklace, the return half of her ticket from Bournemouth to London, and a railway station cloakroom ticket.

Discovered

A trip to the station revealed the suitcase and its incriminating contents. Clothing carrying name tags for 'Heath', a hat and scarf, both stained with blood which was later proven to be that of Margery Gardner and, perhaps even more critical, a riding crop with a diamond pattern that would match the whip marks on the body of the victim. A scarf soaked in saliva was also found and was presumably used to gag Margery Gardner, explaining why no screams were heard on the night of her murder. The game was up. Later that evening, Heath confessed to his identity and was taken to London, charged with murder. But there was still no sign of Doreen Marshall.

Days later, whilst Heath was still denying murder, the body of Doreen Marshall was discovered by a lady walking her dog. Hidden in the bushes, Doreen's clothing, all except for one yellow shoe, had been removed and apparently without any resistance. However, apart from marks suggesting she had been bound by the hands, her head had been battered, a nipple had been bitten off (a clear similarity with the Margery Gardner murder), a slit ran from her stomach to each breast forming a Y-pattern and, what finally killed her, her throat had been stabbed twice. Another inescapable similarity with the Gardner murder was the fact that an instrument had been thrust into her private parts, causing significant damage. Her handbag, stripped of its contents, lay nearby. It was later discovered that Heath had pawned a ring and watch belonging to the late Doreen Marshall.

The hallmarks of these two cases were indisputably too similar to be coincidence and Heath had been implicated beyond any doubt with both women before their untimely deaths.

Trial and execution

On 24th September 1946, Heath was put on trial at the Old Bailey. He instructed his defence counsel to plead not guilty. When

The crowd gathered at the prison gates.

his advisor explained that the evidence against him was overwhelming, he apparently said, 'Then put me down as guilty, old boy!' His lawyer took the decision to enter a plea of insanity and not to allow Heath to speak in his own defence. He could only make matters worse. It didn't help his case when the expert witness who explained how he considered Heath to be insane, was clearly under the influence of drugs whilst giving evidence and it later transpired that he was a drug addict.

Two prison officers, however, were able to contradict the insanity plea, claiming that although he may have been a sexually-motivated psychopath, he knew exactly what he was doing and was not insane. In less than an hour, the jury returned a verdict of guilty and Heath was sentenced to death by hanging.

On 16th October, 29-year-old Heath was hanged by the infamous Albert Pierrepoint. A cool character right to the end, when he was asked if he would like a stiff drink just before his execution, Heath said he'd like a whisky and added 'I think I'll make it a double.'

THE NATION'S MOST HAUNTED HOUSE?

Sandford Orcas Manor

This fine manor house, just a few miles to the north of Sherborne, was built on an ancient Saxon site in 1540. Late Tudor in style and built from the honey-coloured Ham stone, it has fine mullioned windows and gargoyles which stare down ominously as though challenging the presence of any passer-by. Its situation next to the village church and its graveyard further add to its mysterious nature.

It was owned by the Knoyle family until the mid-18th century when a succession of farmers took up the lease, the first of these

Sandford Orcas Manor (Courtesy of Mike Searle)

being John Davidge. At the end of the First World War, the property passed into the hands of the Medlycott family who leased it to Colonel and Mrs Claridge from 1965 to 1979, and they were perhaps the most perceptive to its hauntings, claiming at least fourteen different spirits sharing the premises.

That's what sets this ancient home apart from its rivals, the sheer number of different ghosts. One of the more sinister of these is the 7-ft-tall footman who enters the grounds via the gatehouse and then wanders throughout the manor. He is simply retracing the steps he made whilst preying on the poor servant girls during his mortal time on the premises, knocking on their bedroom doors as he passed. Having moved on, he leaves a vapour trail with the stench of rotting flesh, earning himself the nickname of the 'Stinking Man'. Legend claims that he seduced or raped every girl who worked on the premises but now he only appears to virgins who will hear the sound of him dragging a body along the corridors. But perhaps, again, it is the ghost of a man who once murdered his employer. With so many ghosts, it's difficult to know exactly who's who.

Equally sinister is the priest whose ghostly presence is felt when it tries to smother guests as they sleep in their beds! This is certainly one of those places where it's best to keep the light on when you retire for the night. A lady guest saw a phantom swinging at the foot of her bed in what used to be the nursery room. Having finished his playtime, the evil-faced apparition, wearing evening dress, stood and stared for a while before disappearing. The solarium was regularly visited by a friendly lady spirit when it was the bedroom of a young lad, and others claim to have seen two female ghosts in the same room.

Colonel Claridge was once visited seven nights in a row by a ghost he referred to as 'The Moor'. After a week's visitations, it was not seen again until the same time the following year when once again it stared down at the Colonel and his wife in their four-poster bed. After a bit of research, the Colonel was able to discover that a Moor servant had once been employed at the manor and had murdered his master by putting a length of wire around his throat.

Colonel Claridge also saw a gypsy lady wandering across his lawns well after the gates had been closed. Annoyed by the unwelcome intrusion, he went out to ask what she was doing there, only to see her simply fade away.

Suicides

A frequent visitation comes from the ghost of a former tenant farmer, almost certainly James Davidge, who is seen peering through the kitchen window or walking across the lawns wearing the traditional farmer's hat and white milking smock. He is believed to have committed suicide by hanging himself from a pulley in the gatehouse archway, where his body is still occasionally seen. Many individuals have seen his ghost wandering the grounds and that includes a BBC cameraman who was there to produce a programme on the manor's numerous hauntings.

It appears the gatehouse archway is a popular spot for suicide hangings. The ghost of the nobleman Sir Hubert Medlycott, who is also reputed to have hanged himself from the arch, haunts the grounds.

Ladies in different colours

Mrs Claridge once witnessed an elderly lady dressed all in red on her way up the stairs from the Great Hall. Her presence could have been perfectly natural except for the way she passed through an unopened door into another room. Then there is the 'Lady in White' who uses the stairs and whose presence is accompanied by music emanating from an empty room, not to mention the lady in green and the lady in Elizabethan clothes.

Numerous members of the Knoyle family have appeared from time to time, recognisable from the portraits hung in the house, including Edward Knoyle and a son of the family wearing a Stuart hat.

The insane sea cadet

Around the back of the manor house is a door with an observation panel built in, of the kind that would be at home on the door of a prison cell. Its origins date back to the time when a young sea cadet was deemed to be insane and was kept confined within.

The lad concerned had shown great potential to make a successful naval officer and had been sent to Dartmouth College. Whilst he was there, he killed another cadet, was tried and found to be insane. Returned to Sandford Orcas, he was locked up in the room at the back of the manor. His manic cries could be heard, especially during the hours of darkness when the moon was waxing. Apparently when the moon permitted, the lad was allowed to wander the village at will. In his late twenties, he died and was buried in the grounds of the manor, but his pitiful cries can still be heard when the moon is in the right phase. In more recent times, a young man visited the manor and asked if it was possible to view the room concerned. Permission granted, he entered the room but made a rapid exit, clearly in a state of terror. It took some while for him to regain his composure and when he did, he related how a man had rushed at him with a knife in an attempt to kill him. Was this the re-appearance of the sea cadet and was this how he had killed his fellow cadet?

Fact or fantasy?

Now here comes the real mystery. At the end of the period of the Claridges' lease, the Medlycott family returned to the manor. There are members of that family who claim that in all the decades of their occupation, not one ghost was ever seen; nor has there been a sighting since they moved back in. Yet during the time that the Colonel and his wife were there, the ghostly appearances were so active that the manor could claim to be the nation's most haunted house.

So, is it the house that is haunted or the Claridges? The mystery remains. Is Sandford Orcas the nation's most haunted house? Or did the ghosts take their leave when the last tenants took theirs?

THE HAIR-FETISH MURDERS

Death of a seamstress

Heather Barnett had grown up in the North Dorset town of Sturminster Newton and, aged 48, was now living in Bournemouth. Tuesday, 12th November 2002, had begun just like any other day for Heather and her two children, 11-year-old Caitlin and 14-year-old Terry. By the end of the day, however, the life of this happy family was to be shattered forever in the most horrific way. Heather had given her children their breakfast and driven them to the local Summerbee school at 8.30 am, returning home ten minutes later. She settled in for the day at their ground floor flat in Capstone Road, in the Charminster district of Bournemouth, where she worked long hours as a seamstress. The first awareness of the horrors of that day appeared when the children returned home just after 4 pm.

Terry felt uneasy. There was an unnatural silence in the home and there was no sign of their mother. They called out to her but there was no response. Terry went to his bedroom, changed out of his school clothes and asked his sister where their mother was. Caitlin went to the bathroom and knocked on the door. There was no reply

Heather Barnett

Danilo Restivo.

so she gently pushed the door open. Her reaction was predictable – she had just seen the mutilated body of her mother on the bathroom floor. Terry entered the bathroom to discover that there was blood everywhere. He knew instinctively that this was no accident. He made the 999 call, reported that his mother had been murdered and the two of them went to wait outside the flat pending the arrival of the police. Just at that moment, neighbours from across the road arrived and offered some comfort to the two children. They were Sicilian-born Danilo Restivo and his wife Marsango.

When the police examined Heather's body, they found that her head had been hit several times with a hammer or similar instrument, her throat had been slashed, her body mutilated and then dragged into the bathroom. In her right hand was a clump of hair which was not her own – nor, it would turn out, was it her murderer's, but the hair from another unidentified women who had also fallen foul of the killer but probably in less dramatic circumstances. Heather's hair had also been cut and a chunk placed beneath her other hand. Her bra had been cut open at the front. Further horrific mutilation of her body had taken place. The loss of a mother is tragic at any time, but one can only imagine the impact of that devastating scene on her two children.

As it happened, the cut bra and in particular the hair, provided vital clues leading to the eventual arrest and conviction of the killer. Could the killer have a hair fetish? But first we need to wind the clock back to September 1993.

The Italian Connection

Elisa Claps was a 16-year-old schoolgirl living in the southern Italian town of Potenza. Danilo Restivo had arranged to meet her in the Holy Trinity church. He was the last person to see her alive. It was 12th September and Elisa had completely disappeared. Searches and enquiries all proved fruitless. Danilo, being the last to see her, was clearly in the frame but with no body and no real evidence, there was little the police could do. They interviewed him regarding her disappearance and found inconsistencies in his statements. In March 1995, he was tried by the court and found guilty – of lying to the investigators!

In 2002, Restivo left his home country of Italy and moved to Bournemouth to develop a relationship with Fiamma Marsango, a woman he met on the Internet. The couple lived immediately opposite Heather's ground floor flat. Indeed, Restivo's lounge window looked directly onto the flat where she carried out her work as a seamstress. It was here that he began to plan Heather's murder and from where he carried out a number of hair-fetish attacks in the Bournemouth area.

The day of the murder

In November 2002, Heather Barnett was somewhat disturbed by a visit to her flat by Restivo. His apparent innocent enquiry regarding the possible purchase of curtains had left her unnerved, especially when she realised that a copy of her keys to the flat had disappeared. Heather even wrote to Restivo's wife enquiring whether it was possible that he may have found them. We now know that he was already planning her murder.

On the day of the murder, Restivo bought a bus ticket in the morning and then falsified the time records at his place of employment. Both of these actions were part of his plan to create a false alibi. Some assumptions have to be made as to what happened next. Either Restivo visited Heather who allowed him to enter her flat or, perhaps more likely, he used the spare set of keys to let himself in. Sitting at her place of work, he approached her from behind, attacked her with the blunt instrument, dragged her dead body to the bathroom and placed a lock of someone else's hair in her hand. Using Luminol, a forensic tool which highlights spots of blood, the police later discovered blood-stained footmarks moving backwards, each print fainter than the last, until they ceased abruptly, as though the killer had changed footwear.

The police had their suspicions concerning Restivo. After days of house-to-house enquiries, they searched his home where they found a pair of trainers soaking in bleach, a method known to destroy DNA evidence. He was arrested but released after questioning as they lacked the evidence to convict him. By the spring of 2003, he was still their only suspect and they were convinced he was the killer but he remained at large, a menace to the women of Bournemouth, because of insufficient evidence.

Hair-cutting

During the spring of 2004, there was a spate of attacks on women. A man would approach them from behind and cut off a chunk of hair. The police believed that Restivo was the culprit and were keeping him under covert observation as he frequented secluded parks and public spaces. They were sufficiently concerned about his behaviour that they called for uniformed police to search his car on the pretext that a number of robberies from cars had taken place in the area. He was agitated and sweating heavily, perhaps from fear of being discovered for his crimes, including that of murder. Asked to explain his presence in the car park, he said he was just there for a walk. Inside his car they found scissors and a large knife with a narrow blade, of the kind used for filleting. There was also waterproof clothing with a balaclava helmet and gloves in the pocket. Two pairs of scissors in the driver's door provided another clue as to his possible activities.

An appeal on BBC's *Crimewatch* featuring the hair-fetish attacks brought forward a number of victims who were able to describe Restivo. He was arrested but released. He was arrested again in November 2006 when his home was searched and a lock of hair found. He claimed it had been planted there by the police.

Later in their investigations, faint traces of blood were discovered inside the trainers which had been held by the police. A blood-stained towel had been found at the scene of the crime, apparently, and somewhat carelessly, left behind by the killer. It wasn't until 2008 though that a DNA profile could be found matching Restivo's. Even then, Restivo was attempting to lie his way out of trouble, claiming that he had given the towel to Heather Barnett to provide a colour-match for the curtains he required.

The years ticked by and then came a breakthrough. In March 2010, the body of the Italian girl Elisa Claps was finally found in the bricked-up loft of the same church where she had met Danilo Restivo. It was seventeen years after her disappearance. Her hair had been cut and locks left adjacent to her body; her bra had been cut at the front and her body repeatedly stabbed and mutilated. The similarities between the two murders were all too apparent once the connection between them had been made. The killer was clearly leaving his signature trademark and there was sufficient evidence to link the two cases. The investigating team finally had enough evidence for a prosecution, bringing their eight-year investigation to an end.

On 20th May, 2010, riot vans and squad cars drove into Chatsworth Road, Charminster. There Danilo Restivo was arrested, taken to Poole police station and charged with the murder of Heather Barnett.

Brought to trial

He was brought to trial at Winchester Crown Court. In the public gallery were members of Heather Barnett's family, along with Filomena, the mother of Elisa Claps, who had travelled from her home in Italy. Expert after expert provided evidence regarding DNA and blood analysis. Women whose hair had been cut without their permission, mostly on buses but even in a cinema, all contributed to the evidence put before the jury. Restivo confessed to the jury that he had cut women's hair both in Italy and in England, although denying the murder of Heather Barnett.

Reports of the police surveillance activity were given. The prosecution described how Restivo had worn gloves and had changed his trainers at the scene of the crime in order to avoid detection. Details unfolded of the close relationship developed with the Italian investigation team, some of whom travelled to Winchester to provide vital evidence. Other Italian witnesses and experts gave evidence from Potenza, Salerno and Bologna, taking advantage of video links between the courts. The jury were told how Restivo had been responsible for the death of Elisa Claps and the overwhelming similarities between the two cases were detailed. It was pointed out to the jury that Restivo was only on trial for the murder of Heather Barnett. A trial still awaited in Italy for the murder of Elisa Claps.

The evidence was sufficient to prove that Restivo had carried out the murder and that it had been cold and callous in both the planning and execution: the assumed theft of the keys, the phoney bus ticket, the falsified time records at his place of work. The nature of the murder and the treatment of the body, the placing of the hair all pointed to a seriously deranged and dangerous predator. Throughout the investigation and trial, Restivo's evidence had been contradictory. In his defence, he tried to convince the jury that his medication caused lapses of memory.

On 29th June 2011, at Winchester Crown Court, the years of endeavour by Dorset's Major Crime Investigation team, with help from their Italian counterparts, came to a conclusion. It had proved to be one of the most complex cases ever to challenge the Dorset police force. Thirty-nine-year-old Danilo Restivo was found guilty of murder by the jury at the end of a six-week trial. He was sentenced to a 'whole-life' term in prison, the normal 30-year maximum being felt to be inadequate. Society needed to be protected.

It had taken almost nine years to bring him to justice and to provide some little comfort to Caitlin and Terry who had lost a devoted and hard-working mother.

In a further twist to this story, when 26-year-old Jong-Ok Shin was stabbed three streets away from Restivo's home, a different man was arrested and eventually jailed. His lawyers have instigated an appeal. But what is their justification? Two clumps of hair were found at the scene.

To the Manor Born

It is so easy to envy those born into a privileged society, with that silver spoon in their mouth and the grand manor house to live in. But such privilege comes at a price. There is the cost of the upkeep of such properties and the problem of having to share it with the almost inevitable ghost. The older and larger the building, the more certain you can be that it will house a paranormal presence. Dorset, with its many fine manor houses, is no exception to that rule. Indeed, Sandford Orcas Manor, which we have already mentioned, can claim to provide us with the nation's most haunted house. But there are plenty of others available.

Athelhampton House

Just outside Dorchester lies Athelhampton House, on the eastern edge of Puddletown. In private ownership for over 500 years, it offers hospitality for functions such as civil weddings. Its Great Hall dates back to 1485, when it was surrounded by a 160-acre deer park. It is at the very heart of the house, the home of Sir William Martyn. Once it would have been the one and only room, providing the living quarters for all the family. Over the centuries, the building has been expanded to provide the magnificent house we see today. Once in a while, it will be used as the backdrop for a film or TV series, including the 1972 film, *Sleuth* and TV's *Doctor Who*. Set in its own estate and gardens, its graceful appearance belies a sinister past, just as sinister as any episode from the Doctor! But perhaps more relevant is the fact that it was once the subject of the TV series *Most Haunted*.

Yvette Fielding, the former *Blue Peter* presenter, a medium and a parapsychologist all spent 24 hours there, along with a film crew of fifteen people. The experts claimed to have witnessed spectral orbs near the dungeon and, with such a large film crew, there were plenty of witnesses to the way the orbs appeared to react with the people present. Some even claimed to have seen an orb in the main

Athelhampton House (courtesy of John Lamper).

hall in the shape of a monkey. It is the monkey which is perhaps Athelhampton's best known ghost.

In the 15th/16th century, the daughter of the Martyn family owned a monkey. Legend tells that the monkey was accidentally trapped in a cellar when the building was sold to a new owner. Another version tells how the daughter suffered a broken heart, locked herself and the monkey in a room and committed suicide. The poor monkey starved to death. No one knows for sure which version is closest to the truth. The monkey's ghost is now said to spend its time haunting the house, looking for the latest owner to discover its whereabouts. Its scratching sounds can also be heard coming from behind wooden panelling. As if to add credence to this tale, in St Mary's church in Puddletown, in the south transept, known as the Athelhampton transept, there is a table tomb beneath the arch which dates back to the 15th century. It is carved with the effigy of Sir William Martyn and his feet rest on a grinning monkey.

Amongst the other paranormal guests is a cooper (a barrel maker), whose tapping sounds can be heard in the wine cellar. Of a more violent nature is the pair of duellists who haunt the Great Chamber. One visitor, who was sitting quietly in the Great Chamber, trying to read a book, was so disturbed by these two 'skylarkers' as she saw them, that she promptly told them in no uncertain terms to stop their shenanigans. They continued as if completely unaware of her presence until one of them suffered a cut to the arm, at which point they stopped fighting and left the room. Having been ignored by the duellists, the lady took the matter up with her host who was able to tell her that she was the only other person in the house.

The inevitable Grey Lady is another regular sighting, passing through the walls of the upstairs rooms. Whilst the Grey Lady wanders mostly at night, the Black Priest seems to prefer daylight.

Stalbridge Park

Stalbridge Park lies just outside the village of Stalbridge, close to the Somerset border. All that remains of this once grand estate are the five miles of 10-ft-high walls which once surrounded the grounds of the fine manor house. The house was built in 1638 for Richard Boyle, first Earl of Cork. In 1752 and 1820, it changed hands, being sold to different families. In 1820 it belonged to Henry William Paget, Earl of Uxbridge and Marquis of Anglesey, and it was in that year that it burnt down, being totally demolished two years later. By 1827, all that was left was a large raised piece of ground and the ghost of 'the fiery lady'.

The story goes that during its heyday, the owner of the house would occasionally let other people use it for their own family purposes. One such person was a lady who had been granted permission to use it for her family over the Christmas festive season. She had a large and young family who were going to have great fun in the large house and ample grounds. All she had to promise was that she would do exactly as the housekeeper requested. This she agreed and the only condition the housekeeper put on her was that no one was to be in the Great Hall at five o'clock in the afternoon.

The promise was conscientiously adhered to until the day came when another family joined them. In the latter part of the afternoon, and shortly before five o'clock, the visiting family departed and the lady host bid them goodbye in the hall. As she was about to shut the door, she heard the clock chime five. It was time for her to leave. Alas, she was too late. As she looked up the staircase, she could see the ghost of a lady pass through a bedroom door, completely engulfed in flames. A voice repeatedly cried out 'I have done it!' before the fiery lady disappeared through a different door.

The visiting lady went up the stairs and checked the two doors concerned. Each was securely locked. Being of an inquisitive nature, she returned the following day to see if the apparition repeated itself – and it did. Having convinced herself that the house was haunted, she gathered her family together, packed their bags and departed as fast as she could. With her family safely home, she contacted the owner of the house to let him know what had happened. The explanation behind the ghostly apparitions was then revealed.

The fiery lady

Many years before, the occupants of the house were a widow and her son. The estate employed a gamekeeper whose daughter was in the same age range as the widow's son. The two fell in love but when the widow discovered the affair, she told her son, in no uncertain terms, that the affair was to cease immediately. The gamekeeper's daughter was well beneath his station and the affair could only lead to his ruin.

The couple were not to be put off and the young man informed his mother of their intention to marry. His mother's reaction was predictable and she refused even to listen. His persistence was so annoying that the widow decided that she had to convince her son that his plan was sheer folly. When he eventually announced that he had already married the girl several weeks before, she threw him out of the family home, no doubt hoping that a dose of the real world would bring him to his senses.

As the months passed, and she became more attuned to the *fait accompli*, she sent for her son with a message to return home. She was prepared to forgive and forget and both her son and his wife would be welcomed to live with her at Stalbridge House. For the young couple, life was on the up. The young bride and her mother-in-law got on really well. The girl was charming, witty and good company for the widow, but beneath the surface, bitterness lingered within the widow's heart.

Life took a sad turn when the son returned from a day's hunting to be told that his wife had died in tragic circumstances. It was approaching time for the evening meal and the young wife had dressed for the occasion, the dress blossoming out from the waist into a full flair. She went into her mother-in-law's dressing room and stood before the fire for warmth as she chatted. All at once, having stood too close to the naked flames, she let out a terrifying scream as her dress burst into flames, engulfing the girl from head to foot. The widow explained how there had been nothing she could do. It was all over so quick.

And that could have been the end of the story except that, on her death bed, the widow confessed her sins, one of which was that she had deliberately pushed her daughter-in-law into the flames. What had been accepted as an accident was finally revealed as murder. All that now survives is the ghost of the burning girl and the voice of the widow declaring her guilt.

Corfe Castle – stabbed in the back!

What self-respecting castle doesn't have a ghost or a decent murder story? Corfe Castle is no exception and, once again, family infighting lies at the very heart of the story. King Edgar of England, known as Edgar the Peaceful, was just sixteen when he came to the throne, despite which he proved to be a strong leader. He had two sons: the first, whom some claim was illegitimate, was Edgar whose mother was Elfleda. When she died, Edgar married Elfrida who bore him another son Ethelred. King Edgar was just 32 years old when he died and this left the problem as to which son should take the crown.

Edward was just 13 years old, his younger half-brother was only seven. Edgar had declared that his eldest son, albeit possibly illegitimate, was older and wiser and should be the next king and his wishes were granted. He assumed the role in AD 975. Both children meanwhile were left in the care of the surviving wife, Elfrida. However, Elfrida had ambitions for her own son and plotted Edward's overthrow. In the background, the nation was divided on religious grounds. The late Edgar had leaned towards Rome and its views. The new King Edward also held the same allegiance, whilst the scheming Elfrida, along with her son Ethelred, supported the opposing faction, perhaps in the hope that they would help her to gain the throne for her natural son whom she argued held the legitimate claim to the throne.

Edward, aware of the conflict, worked hard to try and please his stepmother. He was a likeable character, with many of his father's leadership qualities. He even granted her the county of Dorset and she took up residence at Corfe Castle, preferring to stay away from the royal court. This gave her the space and freedom to plot against the king. The opportunity came at the end of a day's hunting. Fresh from the chase in the forest around Corfe, King Edward paid a visit

The murder of Edward the Martyr, from a woodcut by William Harvey, 1835.

to Corfe Castle to visit his step-mother and half-brother. Leaving the hunting party, he travelled alone to the castle and was greeted with deceptive warmth and affection. Remaining mounted, Elfrida offered him a drinking cup which he took. As Edward drank, one of her attendants, commanded by Elfrida, stabbed him in the back. Edward spun his horse around to escape any further attack and headed into the woods. Overcome by loss of blood, he passed out, fell from his horse with his foot still in the stirrup. By the time the horse came to a standstill, Edward was dead. His body was found and carried to the humble cottage of a woman who lived nearby.

The following morning, Elfrida's followers discovered the whereabouts of the body and had it thrown into a marsh. The body was later recovered and afforded a more dignified burial with full royal honours at Wareham, and later buried again at Shaftesbury. Edward was awarded the status of martyr. Meanwhile, Ethelred was crowned king but his reign remained tarnished by the blood of his half-brother. Guilt got the better of his mother and she took holy vows and retired to a priory.

The castle remains that we see today are not those witnessed by Edward. The castle was rebuilt after the Norman Conquest and became a place to fear during the reign of the evil King John. Twenty-two French prisoners of war, knights from Poitou, were left there to starve to death. When William de Braose fell out with King John, he fled to France. King John held William's wife and daughter as hostages, declaring they would starve to death if William didn't surrender himself. They starved to death! Is it any wonder then that the castle ruins are still haunted?

Strange Burials

The misplaced skull

St Nicholas church at Studland is one of Dorset's finest examples of Norman architecture with its unusually stumpy tower. The possible lack of height may have something to do with its weak foundations. Built on sandy soil, the tower was found to be 11 inches out of kilter. Christianity on the site dates back to around the 7th century and the original church here was once destroyed by Vikings. Excavations inside the church revealed burials dating to pre-Christian times. This, once again, shows how Christian churches were often built on sacred pagan sites. With so much history, anything can turn up once the digging starts.

Despite the sandy nature of the soil, the churchyard ground was quite hard in January 1951 when the gravedigger began to excavate a grave. He reached a point a few feet down when his spade hit something solid. It turned out to be a stone slab. Having raised the slab he realised that he had uncovered a stone-built coffin. Inside was the skeleton of a woman, aged about 30 when she died. What was unusual was the way the body had been laid out. Her skull had been separated from the body and the jaw placed behind the skull. A spindle made of shale from Kimmeridge and sea shells accompanied the body. The evidence was similar to Bronze-Age burials found elsewhere in the county.

As far back as the Bronze Age, people feared ghosts and one way to prevent a tormented soul from returning to haunt you was to remove the head, typically placing it by the feet. But that would not stop the spirit's voice from haunting you. Hence the jaw would be removed just to make doubly sure.

Maiden's Grave Gate

On West Creech Hill, to the east of Tyneham, is a road junction known as Maiden's Grave Gate. Near it stands a Coffin Tree, so-called because of the shape of a coffin carved into its bark. It records the 18th-century burial on this Purbeck Hill site where the young dairymaid Jane Gilbert was buried. Her life was cut tragically short when she committed suicide. Crossed in love, she sank into despair and could fathom no other way out of her pain. She hanged herself from a beam in the cowsheds where she worked.

The custom in those times was that suicides could not be buried in hallowed ground. It was normal, indeed it was the law, to bury them at a convenient point just outside the parish boundary, typically at a crossroads. Her body, once placed in the grave, would have had a wooden stake hammered through the chest before being covered over. Two coffins were then carved into the tree. This somehow prevented the spirits from wandering.

The villainous vampire

All counties have their ghost stories to tell – but few can lay claim to a possible vampire in their midst? Dorset has its own unique story of life beyond the grave and it features the once grand residence at Eastbury House, near Tarrant Gunville, north of Blandford Forum, and its steward William Doggett.

Doggett was not the kind of man you would trust to run either your domestic or business affairs whilst you were away abroad. But that, for some foolish reason, was exactly what George Bubb Dodington, the first Baron Melcombe managed to do. The story begins when Bubb Dodington became incredibly rich on inheriting his uncle's estate. With that wealth, in 1718, he commenced the building of a fine mansion at Eastbury Park, third only in grandeur to Blenheim Palace and Castle Howard. It took decades to build. However, the cost of maintaining the property was enormous and became a drain on his resources. At one time he even offered to let it free to anyone prepared to maintain it – but there were no takers.

Bubb Dodington had health problems and for that reason he spent considerable time in Italy and was hardly ever home to oversee his Dorset estate. He was very successful in business and undoubtedly much of his success can be attributed to the corrupt practices for which he was renowned. Perhaps that is why he felt comfortable with his choice of William Doggett as his steward, Doggett being equally corrupt. Doggett was well known to the locals and they predicted that his appointment would end in disaster.

From his home in Italy, Bubb Dodington sent messages to Doggett regarding the estate and when it became clear that the cost of maintenance was untenable, he instructed Doggett to have two of its wings demolished. Meanwhile, Doggett's brother was in deep financial difficulties and Doggett saw the opportunity to clear his brother's debts whilst lining his own pockets at the same time. Rather than just demolish part of the property, he decided to demolish the lot. He was absolutely confident that Bubb Dodington's health was so bad that he would never return to England and so his dishonesty would never be uncovered. The demolition work began but not until everything of any possible value had been removed and sold to Doggett's advantage.

Life was on the up for Doggett but then came the unexpected news that Bubb Dodington had returned and had just alighted from the London mail coach. Doggett's dishonest activities were soon exposed and Bubb Dodington was justifiably furious and demanded repayment of all the monies which Doggett had acquired. But there was none to give. His brother's debts had been cleared and what little was left was insignificant. Bubb Dodington arranged for Doggett to be arrested and tried. On the eve of what would have been his arrest, 23rd June 1786, Doggett could see no way out and went into what remained of the house, loaded a pistol and blew out his brains. Legend has it that the blood stains on the marble floor could never be removed – but even stranger events were yet to happen.

Although the tradition was that suicides should be buried at a crossroads and never in consecrated ground, for some reason, and to the annoyance and fear of the residents, Doggett was buried in the grounds of the parish church at Tarrant Gunville. Their fears were based on the superstition that a suicide buried in consecrated ground would become a vampire.

Ten weeks later, there was an entry in the *Salisbury and Winchester Journal* announcing the sale of goods from the estate of William Doggett (deceased). Various beds, curtains, mattresses, blankets, book cases, wardrobes, bureaux, dining and other tables, chairs and an almost endless list, indeed of such a length that the auctioneer had allocated five days for the disposal of all the goods. We can only assume that these were the spoils of his plundering.

With a Christian burial, in consecrated ground, perhaps the spirit of William Doggett should have laid at rest, but not so. Those who have seen Doggett's wandering spirit describe how a ghostly carriage arrives at Eastbury Park, driven by a headless coachman. A wigged gentleman stands at the gates wearing a yellow ribbon around the legs of his breeches. It is the ghost of Doggett. The coach pulls up alongside him, the coachman asks 'Where to, sir?', the gentleman answers 'Home' and climbs aboard. Taking the coach right up to the ruins of the house, the headless coachman waits as Doggett alights, enters the house and there, to the sound of a pistol shot, repeats his act of self-destruction.

If that in itself is not a sufficiently bizarre story, the sequel almost defies belief. In 1845, some 60 years after Doggett's suicide, Tarrant Gunville church was rebuilt. The work required a number of previous burials to be exhumed and re-buried, including the grave of William Doggett. To the amazement of those involved, when Doggett's body was recovered, there around his legs was tied a yellow ribbon, as crisp and bright as the day it was made, and just as seen on his ghost. Even more amazing, his body showed no signs of decay, his cheeks as perfect and rosy as they had been in life, despite the path of entry and exit of the bullet which killed him being clearly visible.

Tarrant Gunville residents feared for their safety and could only ponder what visitation they may experience once the sun went down and the un-dead took the stage. The body of William Doggett was treated in the traditional way for a vampire, a stake through the heart, and re-buried. Peace returned to the village, his ghost was seen no more and the residents of Tarrant Gunville were unmoving in their belief that their community had harboured a vampire.

Lady Killers

The killer and the cook

'This is Orson Welles speaking from London: The Black Museum, repository of death. (Pause for effect and to hear Big Ben slowly chime). Here in a grim stone structure on the Thames, which houses Scotland Yard, there is a warehouse of homicide, a very strange room where everyday objects: a woman's shoe, a tiny white box, a quilted robe – all are touched by murder.'

These words, against a background of ominous, threatening music, were spoken by one of the great actors of the time. This was how he opened the weekly episode of Radio Luxembourg's *The Black Museum.* He then took the listener on a tour through the museum where Scotland Yard held a collection of artefacts linked to famous cases which they had solved. Orson Welles picked up one of those artefacts, one of those vital pieces of evidence which had led to the discovery of a killer. He then took the listener into the terrifying world of the most heinous of crimes – murder. In an episode from 1952, he picked up a telegram, read the message and related the story of a Dorset murder.

Bogus telegrams

Telegrams tend to have the same effect as pairs of police officers arriving at your door. Imagine – the doorbell rings; you open the door and there before you are two police officers, not one but two. Thoughts of every possible disaster rush through your mind. The natural assumption is that they are the bearers of catastrophic news. When the post boy arrived at the door with the telegram in the brown envelope, the effect was just the same, especially in the war years when so many were delivered. But telegrams can also be the bearers of good news, the announcement of a new arrival, the successful reply to a job application. They could also be a trap, a lure to a fatal encounter. That was the case in December 1921 when a Boscombe resident was luring unsuspecting women into his trap.

It was Saturday, 17th December 1921. Thomas Henry Allaway had picked up his copy of *The Morning Post* and an advertisement caught his attention. A 21-year-old trained nurse was seeking a position as a companion nurse/maid. She described herself as refined, with good references and seeking a position in the USA. That afternoon, Thomas Allaway went to the post office at Boscombe and sent a telegram in reply using the name of a Mrs Cooper. It instructed the nurse to take the 4.30 Waterloo train to Bournemouth where she would be met by a driver. Her expenses would be paid and she should be prepared to stay overnight. The telegram was full of spelling errors which was to prove significant in later investigations. Fortunately for the nurse concerned, she decided to ignore the message.

Three days later on the Tuesday morning, Irene May Wilkins, a 31-year-old cook sent the details of an advertisement she wanted entered into *The Morning Post*. It would go into the paper two days later on the Thursday. It gave her age and announced her as an experienced school cook seeking an immediate position. On the same day that she posted her letter, Allaway was back in the Boscombe post office sending another telegram, this time to a London-based employment agency which advertised for nurses in *The Morning Post*. The telegram, signed as from the butler at Boscombe Grange, asked the agency to send a pleasant nurse by the 5.30 Waterloo to Boscombe train. She would be met at the station.

The following day, a nurse by the name of Burnside caught the train but soon faced a series of mishaps. The train actually didn't stop at Boscombe and so she took a taxi from Bournemouth to Boscombe Grange, only to discover that there was no butler there and no one had sent a telegram. Determined not to let the agency down, she booked herself into a B & B and resumed her search in the morning.

Ten o'clock the following morning, she was in the post office from where the telegram had been sent. She used the post office telephone to ring her agency and began to make enquiries about what turned out to be a bogus telegram. She left the post office at about 11 o'clock. During the time that she was there, amazingly, Allaway entered the post office. That morning he had read Irene Wilkins's advertisement in the paper and was sending a reply in the name of Wood of Beech House. Nurse Burnside had just had a close encounter with a killer but by good fortune returned to London unscathed. Irene Wilkins was not to be so lucky.

It was midday the same day when Irene received the telegram apparently from Mr Wood but actually from Allaway. It told her to take the 4.30 train from Waterloo to Bournemouth where a car would meet her. By three o'clock she had packed an attaché case with the minimum amount of overnight clothing, had sent a telegram in reply to confirm she was on her way and caught the train. Just after the train left, her family had a visit from the telegram boy which caused them grave concern regarding her safety. Her telegram had been returned. The address didn't exist.

The victim's body

The following morning, at about 7.30 am, a dog walker discovered a body on a piece of uncultivated ground near Seafield Road in Bournemouth. Clues to her identity came from a watch pinned to the breast of her blouse with the initials 'IMW' and name labels on her clothing showing her to be I. Wilkins. Back at her home, her family had reported her missing and it wasn't long before they knew just who the victim was but not so her killer. Her legs were wide apart, exposing her underwear, albeit no signs of interference. Her face was a mass of congealed blood, her head having suffered violent blows probably from a hammer, leaving a hole right through her skull.

It had clearly been a vicious attack and it became obvious from a trail of blood that she had been dragged across a path and a fence to the concealed position where her body was found. Her blood-stained umbrella and her hat were found nearby. Marks in the mud revealed the prints of a woman's boots, a man's shoes and car tyre marks which were to prove particularly useful. They had the tread which matched them to Dunlop Magnums.

The police soon discovered that Irene had received a telegram and that it had been sent from the Boscombe post office. Their enquiries at the post office led them to the discovery of the two other telegrams that had been sent. The original copies were all held at the post office and were clearly sent by the same person. The handwriting and spelling errors were a dead giveaway. Different counter clerks had been involved in sending off the telegrams but one of them managed to remember the man involved. She described him as dressed in a chauffeur's uniform, with a distinctive husky voice.

The police had their first clue as to the man's identity. They widened their questioning following Irene's probable route, talking to railway staff and taxi drivers. They found two witnesses who had seen Irene get into a blue Sunbeam car and others who described a large grey car.

By now, the press were in full flow. Headlines referring to 'The Christmas Killer' kept the case in the public's eye and further witnesses came forward, but to some extent they were adding to the confusion with conflicting stories, all of which needed to be sorted out. The police were particularly keen to interview all the drivers who had been at the station that day. They knew roughly how many had been there but very few had offered to come forward for interview. The only option was to round them all up, all the drivers and chauffeurs (there weren't that many in 1921!) and interrogate the lot. Amongst them was Thomas Allaway, the chauffeur to a man who lived at Bournemouth's Carlton Hotel. Allaway himself lived at Boscombe with his wife and family. He kept the car in a garage across the road from his home. The police examined it and found that three of the tyres were Dunlop Magnums.

Unreliable alibis

Allaway was a creature of habit. He haunted the same pubs, did the same things on a routine basis. This enabled him to produce a catalogue of false alibis. He could account for his presence at the time of the murder. Witnesses swore that, 'Yes – he was in the pub that evening'. But when questioned at length, the alibis began to fall by the wayside as the witnesses realised that they thought they remembered him in various places but only because he usually was.

One witness proved to be key to the investigation. He had travelled on the same train as Irene. He saw her get off at Boscombe and saw her get picked up by a chauffeur. He gave an accurate and detailed description of the driver. He even gave, with incredible accuracy, a full description of the car driven by the killer. It so happened that the witness was a car designer. Two weeks later, when the same witness was back at the railway station, he saw the same chauffeur with the same car. He took a note of its registration and passed the details on to the police.

Sad to say, his statement got buried in a pile of paperwork and no progress was made in the investigation. The police even used a psychic medium in a desperate attempt to uncover more clues. It was the middle of April before one of the investigators uncovered the hidden statement. It must have been an incredibly frustrating moment, realising that the vital clue had been there all along. They now knew who the killer was. The registration belonged to the car driven by Thomas Allaway.

Meanwhile, Allaway must have felt the police enquiries closing in on him. He sent his wife and children to live with her family in Reading, stole a load of cheques from his employer and headed to the anonymity of life in London. There he was making best use of the cheques and an assumed name. Attempts by the police to track him down were unsuccessful, but the Dorset police asked their colleagues in Reading to keep an eye on the house where his wife was now staying. As good as gold, he turned up the very same evening but quickly spotted that the house was being watched. He made a dash for freedom, easily outrunning the pursuing officer but failed to see the leg that a member of the public deliberately stuck out in front of him. In his pockets were a number of betting slips – and the handwriting matched those on the original telegrams.

Arrested

He was arrested and taken into custody. The witness who saw him at the station identified him in a police line-up and the post office clerk identified him by his distinctive voice at another line-up. His trial took place in early July 1922. He pleaded innocent but the evidence against him was overwhelming. His reaction when the guilty verdict was returned was one of total disbelief and he had to ask to hear it a second time. The penalty, as always in such cases, was death by hanging. On 19th August, he walked to the scaffold where he was met by John Ellis, the hangman, and his assistant Edward Taylor. The previous night he had confessed his guilt to the prison governor.

* * *

The murder in the wood

The Ackling Dyke is a 22-mile section of the old Roman road which runs from Old Sarum to the hill fort at Badbury Rings. Villages lie scattered along its length and two of these are the neighbouring villages of Manswood and Gussage St Mary. It was around these villages that the life of Winifred Mary Mitchell had its beginning and its end.

Winifred Mitchell was born in Manswood in June 1889, one of several children from a large family. She had grown into an attractive young woman, shapely of figure and with a great sense of humour. She had intelligence and charm and had everything going for her. She also had the benefit of experience away from village life. Having gone into service, she had worked for several years in Bournemouth. But, at the age of 23, she returned to the rural community closer to her home, taking up employment as a cook for George Good, the farmer at Manor Farm in Gussage St Mary. It was just two miles, an half an hour's walk, from her home village.

Also working on the same farm, as a rabbit trapper, was 29-year-old William Burton. He cut a fine figure, dressed well, stood erect and could have been taken as a man of substance but nonetheless was simply a humble rabbit trapper. He was also an upstanding member of the community, a regular churchgoer as a chorister and one of the village bell ringers. He and Winifred would have made a fine-looking couple and under normal circumstances it would have surprised no one if they had taken up together. However, William was a married man with children and such behaviour should have been out of the question. His wife was also a respected member of the community as the postmistress and school teacher.

William was not one to allow convention to stand in his way though and, in truth, he was very flirtatious and had had several affairs with women despite his married status. Inevitably, he turned his attention to Winifred and she fell for his charm. Over the months that followed, they wrote love letters to each other and swapped gifts, all under a cloak of secrecy. The clandestine affair had reached a critical stage. Burton wanted more than just mild affection. He intended to take the relationship to the next level but Winifred was protecting her virtue and declined. Burton wrote to her telling her that by not giving into him, she had effectively ended the affair. He wished her well and suggested that he would like to think that when she was in someone else's arms, she would perhaps be thinking of William Burton. What a smoothie! What a charmer! But it had the desired effect and she gave in. He had his wicked way.

Weeks later, Winifred dropped a bombshell when she announced to Burton that she was pregnant. They talked about emigrating to Canada. But it was only talk from Burton, who confided in a friend that he wished he could find someone to take Winifred off his hands. Winifred at the same time was breaking the news to her mother who was shocked at the thought of her daughter going away, and not even knowing where she was going. Elsewhere, Burton was consulting another friend explaining to him how Winifred was going to travel to Wimborne and from there by train to London, where he would meet her. His friend did his best to make Burton see sense and stay, feeling it would all go badly wrong if he walked out on his family.

Burton appeared to have been persuaded by the argument and told Winifred that he had changed his mind. Winifred was horrified. Her world was collapsing around her. She was desperate and threatened to reveal all if Burton did not go through with their plan. She would tell his wife, and not just about his affair with her, but all the other women he had seduced. The whole community would know. He would be disgraced and shunned by the villagers.

Two days later, on Monday 31st March, just after lunch, Winifred donned her Sunday best and by three o'clock was cycling out of the village. She stopped to talk to Burton's wife, as though everything was just as it should be. The two got on quite well, being distantly related. Further on she stopped to talk to Burton himself and was seen by a villager passing by. That villager was significant as a witness because that was the last time anyone other than her killer saw her alive.

Unbeknown to Winifred, shortly before their meeting, Burton had asked a friend if he could borrow a shotgun to kill an aged cat. The friend agreed and Burton then asked him if such a gun could kill a person. It was agreed that it could take someone's head right off. This was about half an hour before Winifred met him. Half an hour after they had been seen together, Burton cycled back into the village and returned the gun, minus one of the cartridges. He then asked his friend not to mention that he, Burton, had used the gun but that in fact the two of them had walked to the top of the nearby hill ridge and he, the friend, had fired the gun. It was a strange and suspicious request, made all the more suspicious when the aged black and white cat was seen, still alive.

Winifred's disappearance was starting to draw attention. Burton was quite actively promoting the rumour that she had gone to London and was contemplating emigration to Canada. Over the following four weeks, his stories changed, even contradicting himself at times, sometimes saying that she had been seen in London, and other times that no one had seen her since she left the village. Then came a breakthrough in discovering the truth.

One of the villagers had found a part of a denture in the woods at Sovel Plantation. Having taken it home, he placed it on the mantelpiece unaware of its significance. The village rector spotted it and immediately made the connection with Winifred. He called the local policeman and the finder explained how and where he had found it. The police enquiries then began unfolding a story. Burton had asked to borrow a gun. Half an hour later he was seen with Winfred. Half an hour after that, Burton was seen cycling away from the plantation and the gun was returned. A witness who saw Burton riding Winifred's bike away was warned by Burton not to open his mouth or else!

The next turning point was the discovery of Winifred's grave. Two young lads told how they had seen a newly-dug grave some weeks before. They guided PC Albert Light and a fellow officer to the spot where, after a bit of probing, they discovered Winifred's body, her head partially blown away. Another piece of false teeth, matching the earlier find, was uncovered. Winifred's mother was only able to identify the body by a button from her coat. From that day on, according to Winifred's sister Lillian, her mother's hair turned white.

Burton was arrested and taken to Cranborne police station. On 7th and 21st May, there were preliminary hearings at Wimborne. So large was the crowd that they couldn't all get in and the police had to take control. There was an equally large turnout at Winifred's funeral on 8th May. The actual trial took place at the Dorset Assizes in Dorchester on 1st June. Burton, smartly turned out, entered a plea of not guilty. Throughout the trial he gave a confident and detailed explanation of his version of events but his facts were undermined by all the others who gave their accounts of Winifred's last day. On the fourth day of the trial, the jury returned their verdict of guilty.

In the three weeks that followed pending his execution, Burton repented. He gave a full confession and took communion. Those weeks also provided sufficient time to erect a new gallows at Dorchester gaol, the old ones not having been used for 26 years.

On 24th June 1913, Burton was led from his cell to the execution platform. With his hands tied behind his back, he followed his chaplain as he walked firmly and erect, in full control of his emotions. Reaching the platform and taking his place on the trap, the black hood was placed over his head, with the noose correctly positioned by Albert Pierrepoint, the executioner. The trap was released and Burton dropped to his death. His body, as was the tradition, was buried within the confines of the prison.

The sad twist to this tale is that at Winifred's post mortem, the coroner revealed that Winifred was definitely not pregnant. Was it her own tangled web that she had woven and into which she had fatally fallen? Or did she genuinely believe that she was pregnant? That is a secret which she sadly took to her grave.

THE MYSTERY OF THE SS *TREVEAL* DISASTER

At first glance, the loss of the SS *Treveal* in 1920 was just another shipping disaster. A closer look at the facts, though, raises a number of serious questions and the mystery is 'Could the disaster of the SS *Treveal* have been avoided?' For instance,

- Why was there such a delay in sending out the Admiralty tug to help the stricken vessel?
- Why didn't it find the vessel when it got there?
- Why wasn't the coastguard's rocket apparatus put into practice to rescue the ship's personnel?
- Why were the coastguard's instructions to the ship's captain so inadequate?
- Why did the ship's captain give the instruction to abandon ship when the seas were too high for the lifeboats?

The questions and the mystery remain.

The SS *Treveal*

The Hain family, based in St Ives, Cornwall, had a long association with ships and the sea. It was their company which was having the new ship built at the Harland and Wolff shipyard in Govan. When her keel was laid down in 1918, she was named the *War Jonquil* and was built to the First World War A-type standard cargo specification. By the time she was launched in June 1919, the war was over and this steam-driven, 400-ft-long, 5,200 tonnage vessel had been named the SS *Treveal*. Her first duty was to bring a cargo of jute and manganese ore from Calcutta to Dundee. Her crew of 43 included eight men from St Ives, one being Captain Charles Paynter. She had sailed all the way back into English waters when, on 9th January 1920, the weather turned for the worse and the tragedy began to unfold.

The captain took the decision to head for the shelter of Portland harbour where he would request the services of a pilot. He arrived just before six o'clock to discover that no pilot was available. He contacted his shipping agent who, somewhat surprisingly, ordered him to carry on without the knowledge and assistance of a local pilot. Two hours later the *Treveal* was heading away from the shelter of Portland, heading into worsening conditions.

The SS Treveal *prior to its first and only voyage.*

As Captain Paynter had anticipated, once he cleared the shelter of Portland Roads, the sea was much rougher and he was struggling to make headway. He made radio contact with Portland to ask for a tug to come to his assistance, only to be told that there wasn't one immediately available but one would be sent out as soon as possible.

Hard and fast on Kimmeridge Ledges

The ship was by now under the control of the sea, the weather and the tides, and being driven towards St Alban's Head. Before long she was grounding on the Kimmeridge Ledges, fingers of limestone rock which reach out into the shallow waters along this coast, to the west of Chapman's Pool. The captain radioed the coastguard to tell him that the *Treveal* was hard and fast aground. He then asked the coastguard to advise him as to whether or not there was a safe landing place nearby. By now it was dark and bitterly cold. The coastguard perhaps believed that they were closer than they actually were to Chapman's Pool, which offered relatively safe landing, rather than where they were off the rocks of Kimmeridge. The problem with Chapman's Pool was that it required good local knowledge of the way that the currents run.

Desperate now for a safe way out, the captain asked what was happening with the expected tug. He asked for the request for the tug to be escalated to the senior officer at Portland. Just before midnight, the tug *Pilot* set out from Portland. The height of the waves was so great that there was no hope of spotting the stranded ship in the darkness. The tug returned to port but set out again about two hours before daybreak and this time was able to find the *Treveal*. Now, however the weather was even worse, with the waves crashing over the shipwrecked vessel. Any attempt to reach the ship would have been potentially disastrous with the tug being smashed against the cargo ship so it was once again forced to return to the harbour.

Meanwhile, other help was on its way. With the assistance of a tug, the 12-oared Weymouth lifeboat was on its way. The combination of the inrushing tide and the heavy seas kept sweeping her past her target. It was beyond the strength of the lifeboat crew to take their vessel within working range of the *Treveal*. Indeed, the seas were so rough that she was even unable to head for her home port and had to seek the safer waters beyond Poole.

On board the *Treveal*, the captain's concern for his crew had reached crisis point. They had been battered by the seas for twelve hours, right through the hours of darkness. It seemed that help would never reach them and they were on their own. He radioed the coastguard for the last time, with desperation in his voice, 'For God's sake, send us assistance!' He signalled to the tug from Portland which was standing by but unable to assist. He took the decision to abandon ship. Two of his lifeboats had already been wrecked by the storm; just two survived. If he lost another, it would be too late. The captain fired their distress rockets and the crew took to the boats. They pulled away from their ship and rowed towards Chapman's Pool, the waves sweeping them forward like surf boards. They were just able to keep control by using the oars. As they approached a slipway, they had to turn sideways on to the waves and that was their undoing. Within seconds they had flipped over, their passengers abandoned to the mercy of the seas.

A 12-oared lifeboat similar to the one that tried to help the Treveal.

Local heroes

Thrown from the lifeboats, their life jackets kept them afloat but the sea was a cruel mistress, sweeping each sailor into the jagged rocks. Their bodies were battered and torn. Horace Piercey, the vicar of Worth Matravers, and Frank Lander, a young fisherman from the village, responded to the distress rocket, running down to the shore where, up to their necks in the sea, they rescued as many as they could. For over an hour, the two brave villagers, bitterly cold, stood in the raging seas, battered by the storm-thrown shingle. They were later awarded the Royal Humane Society's bronze medal.

Only seven of the crew survived, one being a 15-year-old cabin boy. Twenty bodies of the thirty-six who perished were recovered, many of them naked, their clothing ripped off their bodies as the sea battered them against the rocks. Among those who perished was Captain Paynter. Two bodies remained unidentified and were buried in the parish church at Worth Matravers. The others were returned by the steamship company to their family homes.

The unanswered questions

The loss of the ship and the lives of so many of its crew raised a number of questions. In Parliament, Viscount Curzon asked the First Lord of the Admiralty to explain why, when the naval authorities at Portland had been informed at 9.15 in the evening that the *Treveal* was in peril, they had not passed that information on to the lifeboat stations at Swanage and Weymouth until 9.40 the following morning, and why the lifeboat station at Poole hadn't been informed at all, thus explaining why they failed to reach the wreck until 11.30 am. He continued his pointed attack by asking why, despite knowing that the crew were to abandon ship, the coastguard had failed to make any attempt to rescue them. He failed to get any answers other than those that one can expect when the questions cause embarrassment. All he got was the promise of an enquiry. Two weeks later, he raised the question again, this time asking to be told what the result of the enquiry had been. Still no action had been taken.

Thanks to the newspaper headlines following this case, Chapman's Pool acquired the nickname of Deadman's Pool. The chief officer for the coastguard was found guilty of negligence and dismissed from the service. To some extent he was a scapegoat. There were problems in his area of responsibility but there were so many others opportunities missed, any one of which could have given this story a less dramatic, less tragic ending.

Slaughtered by Smugglers

There can be few better places for smuggling along the south coast than around Christchurch harbour, where the rivers Stour and Avon meet as they pour into the natural bay. To the east lies Mudeford with its quay; to the west is Christchurch and the hamlet of Wick, the last village on the Stour and where a punt-ferry service once ran. At the heart of Wick is a small green, with cottages scattered around. It was in this tranquil setting that the 'Wicked Man of Wick' once lived.

Samuel Hookey, the Wicked Man of Wick

Born in 1725, Samuel Hookey was the son of a fisherman. In this part of the world, to be a fisherman was synonymous with being a smuggler. His father, on an excursion to the Channel Islands, apparently abducted a beautiful young Spanish lass and took her for his wife. They had ten children, Samuel being one of them. As a child, he was a bit on the wild side and during one of his childhood escapades, he was digging a tunnel into an ancient burial mound on Hengistbury Head when it collapsed and he lived the rest of his life with a limp.

As far as I know, Samuel never actually killed anyone but I include him here because he was such a colourful character. He was the real McCoy piratic smuggler of the 'Ooh-ar' kind, with a patch over one eye. He lost the eye during one of the many skirmishes in which he was involved. It is alleged that he wore the same eye patch for the rest of his life, never having it cleaned. Apart from smuggling, he managed to conceal his illegal activities by working as a farrier at a blacksmith's workshop.

He was something of a smooth operator, devising cunning plans to confuse the authorities, exploits which would become legend and add to the character's popularity. One example was an episode in 1764. Samuel had four luggers, small-sailed working boats. He ordered one of these to drop a cargo ashore at Bourne Bottom, six miles from Christchurch harbour, along the coast towards Bournemouth. He then tipped off a Riding Officer as to what was going to happen. Riding Officers were government men whose role was to ride their own stretch of coastline watching out for smuggling activity and then communicating that information to their neighbouring customs officers. As the Customs men arrived at Bourne Bottom, Samuel's three other luggers slipped unnoticed into Christchurch harbour.

Meanwhile, the Customs men descended on the crew of the lugger at Bourne Bottom as they brought their barrels ashore. On examination they contained just sea water. As fast as their horses would carry them, the Customs men galloped to Christchurch harbour where Samuel had already successfully tucked away over 12,000 tubs of brandy, a couple of tons of tea and five bales of silk!

At the ripe old age of 71, perhaps he should have hung up his sword and eye patch and settled for a peaceful retirement because Samuel's final smuggling run turned out to be one too many. He was bringing in a cargo of tea and gold when he was ambushed by the Customs men. He jumped over the side of his boat as gunfire poured in on them. He attempted to wade ashore but fell foul of one of the many holes in the bed of the River Stour. Samuel plummeted into the depths, weighed down by the gold in his pockets, never to surface again. Dorset had lost one of its most colourful characters.

* * *

There were many large gangs of smugglers. Quite often small communities would depend on smuggling for their livelihood and hence it was a way of life. It bonded communities together and gang culture was prevalent. In 1748, when the Customs men captured a shipload of contraband, previously in the possession of the Hawkhurst gang from Sussex, they took the spoils to the Customs House at Poole. The audacious gang actually raided the Customs House to retrieve their property. That earned them a price on their heads. The acts of these gangs were full of daring and they were dangerous characters when facing capture, as was the case in the Battle of Mudeford and the skirmish at West Lulworth.

The Battle of Mudeford

There is a narrow entrance to Christchurch harbour called the Run. Being the only entrance, it gives the advantage to the local seamen who know how to pass through and it also acts as a barrier to larger ships which may be in pursuit of smugglers. Needless to say, the Customs men kept a close eye on whatever boats passed through the Run. The smugglers, however, had their own customs-avoidance techniques. Barrels of brandy would be strapped beneath a raft and allowed to drift through the Run on an incoming tide. A strong swimmer would travel with it to steer it on its way, as often as not into Mother Siller's Channel, a creek with runs into the Stanpit Marsh. At the end of this channel was a track which led to an inn, the Ship in Distress, which still exists at Stanpit.

In 1784, Hannah Seller was the landlady of the Ship and was a friend to the smugglers, allowing them to use the Ship in Distress, and another inn in which she had an interest, to store their contraband. When smugglers were in trouble, she would even clear out her law-abiding customers so the smugglers could operate freely. The occasion of the battle, which went down into history, happened when two luggers arrived from the Channel Islands carrying a full cargo of tea and brandy. It was mid-July 1784 and 300 local inhabitants, all of whom benefitted from smuggling, were unloading the cargo on Mudeford beach. Fifty wagons, with six horses to pull each, were being loaded when the navy arrived. HMS *Orestes* and two cruisers appeared from around Hengistbury Head. Once sighted, all hell broke loose on the beach. One of the smugglers went to the nearby inn and rounded up the customers to give the smugglers a hand. The two luggers were brought ashore and contraband was disappearing at a rate of knots. Horse-drawn wagons were galloping off into the distance.

Offshore, the captain of the *Orestes* ordered six boats to be lowered with sailors, armed with rifles and cutlasses, to pursue the smugglers and retrieve whatever could be captured. Approaching the shore, demands to surrender were shouted to the smugglers whose response was to fire a volley of shot across the approaching vessels. William Allen, who had demanded the surrender, fell dead. The sailors on board retaliated and both sides fired at will. Those onshore had the advantage of defensive trenches created for just such an occasion. Those in the bobbing boats had no real cover at all and an unstable base from which to aim. They were relieved to reach the shore, at which point the smugglers retreated to the safety of nearby Haven House where they defended their position for several hours. An attempt to use the guns of the *Orestes* to shell the inn proved disastrous, with their target overshot by some two miles, hitting the distant priory.

The battle over, the two luggers were seized but thousands of gallons of spirits and 25 tons of tea had found their way into the black economy of Christchurch. Three of the smugglers were eventually arrested but two were released, leaving just George Coombes to suffer the wrath of the judicial system. Found guilty, he was hanged and his body suspended in chains at Haven House Point where it served as a salutary message to the customers of the Haven House Inn until, as an act of decency, they cut it down and his friends were able to bury his remains.

Slaughter at West Lulworth

On 28th June 1832, West Lulworth was to witness perhaps the most vicious and callous slaughter of a Customs officer. A narrow stretch of beach separated the sea from the 100-ft-high cliff, providing an ideal spot to bring contraband ashore. Thomas Barrett, a coastguard, was patrolling the cliff top as he walked towards Durdle Door, overlooking St Oswald's Bay. Down below he could see a boat heading westward, as if coming from the Swanage direction. It was ten o'clock in the evening and the light was beginning to fail. If he was to investigate, he would have to move rapidly. He made his way down to the beach where the boat had already landed and was shoving off again, leaving four men standing in the shallows of the beach.

Barrett asked them about the nature of their business and was told that they were just on a trip out of Weymouth, but Barrett had seen them coming from the other direction. Barrett didn't believe them and told them so. With a string of insults aimed at the officer, the four men moved off towards the cliffs. As they headed up the cliff path, Barrett spotted 29 brandy tubs at the landing spot. He lit a blue flare and fired several shots into the air to summon his fellow officers.

Customs men, seeing the alarm, made towards the area and three arrived fairly soon, joining Barrett on the beach. At the same time, an even greater number of locals, sympathetic to the smugglers, moved in to add their support for the offenders. Around 50 locals were at the cliff top to welcome their allies.

Seeing the large number gathered above them on the cliff top, the Customs men moved towards the cliff, putting themselves in a position to protect the barrels until further officers arrived. The opposing groups were about the length of a cricket strip apart. The officers were immediately met with a hail of bullets and stones and an exchange of fire continued in the dim evening light for three quarters of an hour.

The atmosphere changed as the officers heard an agonising cry from the cliff top, followed by near silence as the crowd dispersed. Peace having descended, they returned to the barrels just as another officer, Lieutenant Stocker, arrived by boat. They put the barrels aboard and Barrett was pulling away from the shore when he was called back. An injured man was approaching.

While all of this had been going on, up on the cliff top, two other Royal Navy officers had arrived. Realising what was happening, and despite being outnumbered fifty to two, they had approached the smugglers from their rear. The mob turned on them, viciously beating them with 6-ft clubs. They stood back-to-back fighting with their cutlasses, but were soon beaten down. One of the officers called Duke was beaten incessantly as the mob dragged him by his belt towards the 100-ft cliff. With one man on each limb, and swinging him back and forth to gain momentum, they were just about to launch him when a commanding voice told them to stop.

The voice belonged to one of the mob, James Cowland, whose own life had been saved a year before by the man he had just saved. He was repaying his debt but his help went no further; he walked away. The crowd having dispersed, Duke crawled slowly, making his way down to the beach. On his way, he saw the remains of clothing worn by his officer, Lieutenant Knight, but no sign of the man himself. Reaching the beach, he found Knight, barely alive. Knight, who had been thrown over the cliff, was unable to see and asked if it was Duke who had reached him. They were his final words. Duke hailed his fellow officers on the beach and Knight was loaded into the boat and taken to his West Lulworth home, where he died the following day, aged 42.

A month later, James Davis and Charles Bascombe, were sent for trial for the murder of the officer, amongst numerous other charges. They were both found guilty and suffered the ultimate penalty.

Arsenic in his Oxo

She was young, she was beautiful and she was open to offers. That describes Charlotte McHugh reasonably accurately. Born in Londonderry in 1904, she grew up during the times of the worst of the 'Troubles' in Northern Ireland, when the British army were thick on the ground. At 19 years old, she was the soldier's best friend, openly promiscuous, so much so that the Republican activists threatened her with tarring and feathering for fraternising with the enemy. Amongst the troops serving there was the Dorset Regiment and one of their number was the Military Policeman Frederick Bryant.

Despite her reputation, or maybe because of it, in 1922 Frederick Bryant fell for the girl and when he returned to England, took her with him. His spell in the army over, they got married in Wells and he took up employment as a cowman at Over Compton. It was a small village, quiet and dull in comparison with Londonderry. It was not a lifestyle that suited the still wild and promiscuous Charlotte. She was a regular at the village inn and it appears that although she had no formal employment, she earned a bit on the side by way of prostitution. Her husband, who was quite aware of what was going on, took the attitude that as long as she could earn more than double what he did as a cowman, then he couldn't see a problem. The trouble was that the respectable villagers could.

Towards the end of 1933, Leonard Parsons entered their lives and it was to be a turning point for all concerned. By this time Charlotte had produced five children. Parsons, a horse-trading traveller, had a wife and family of his own but that didn't stop him moving in with the Bryants. Before too long he was sharing Charlotte's bed and her husband was having to sleep on the sofa. But, as long as the money was good...

Bryant's employer found the situation unacceptable, sacked Bryant and kicked him out of his cottage. The couple moved to Coombe, just outside Sherborne. Parsons soon followed and the

Charlotte Bryant, aged 26.

previous arrangement continued whenever he was in the area. The day finally came when Frederick Bryant decided that enough was enough. He told Parsons that his days at the cottage were over. Bryant, however, had not anticipated the outcome. His wife left him and moved into rented accommodation with Parsons but they had problems paying the rent and the two of them moved back in with Frederick Bryant.

Parsons must have decided for himself that it was time to move on and he bid Charlotte farewell. She was devastated and in the days that followed would search the pubs trying to track him

Protesters gathered outside Exeter prison on the day of the execution.

down. Shortly after, Frederick Bryant began to suffer bouts of severe stomach pains, each time after a meal. It happened in May 1835, then in August and again in November. Initially diagnosed as gastro-enteritis by the doctor, the final attack came on 22nd December, just after Charlotte had given him a drink of Oxo, a drink which, it was later established, completely masked the smell of the arsenic. Taken into Sherborne hospital, he died the following morning. The post-mortem revealed that he had died from arsenic poisoning.

The Dorset police put Charlotte and her children into the Sturminster Newton workhouse while they searched the house. There they found the evidence required, primarily a burnt tin which once contained arsenic. Shop-to-shop enquiries eventually discovered a Yeovil chemist who remembered selling her the tin and was able to identify her.

Her trial took place at Dorchester and began on 7th May 1936. After four days of evidence, Charlotte Bryant was found guilty of murder and condemned to death by hanging. Dorchester no longer had provision for executions and so she was taken to Exeter for her final days.

In the six weeks that followed, she maintained that she was innocent. The stress was so great that amazingly the roots of her hair turned from their previous crow-black to white. Her appeal having been turned down, she went to the scaffold, escorted by a Catholic priest, at 8 am on 15th July, where Thomas Pierrepoint performed his duties as executioner. A huge crowd had gathered outside at the appointed hour, voicing their abhorrence of the death penalty.

Aged just 33, she left her worldly wealth of five shillings eight and a half pence to her children who had been taken into care by Dorset County Council.

WAS JACK DRUITT 'JACK THE RIPPER'?

Montague John Druitt was born in Wimborne Minster in August 1857 and died aged 31 in December 1888. He was buried in the town cemetery, having committed suicide just days after Jack the Ripper's last murder. But what could have driven him to such a drastic end? Had he actually been Jack the Ripper? His own family thought so! He was one of the top three suspects and not without good reason.

He had a privileged childhood, his father being a medical practitioner in Wimborne. The family, which included Jack's six brothers and one sister, lived at the spacious Westfield House. Jack was educated at Winchester College and New College, Oxford. At both of these he excelled at sport. He played cricket for Dorset and was very strong around the arms and wrists, being capable of throwing a cricket ball well over 90 yards. He proved himself a very capable debater, taking a strong interest in politics and was well known for his outspoken views. He finally graduated with a degree in classics.

Montague John (Jack) Druitt.

His working life started in 1881 when he taught for a year at a boarding school in Blackheath but the following year he decided that he would follow a career in law. He was admitted to the Inner Temple in 1882 and set up as a barrister when he was called to the Bar in 1885. It was the same year that his father died. Three years later, in the July of 1888, his mother was admitted to a lunatic asylum and perhaps this was a turning point in Druitt's own sanity. The following month, Jack the Ripper struck for the first time. His final victim, Mary Kelly, met her premature end shortly before Jack Druitt's body was found floating in the River Thames, his pockets weighed down with stones. Also in his pockets was a train ticket to Hammersmith and a silver watch on a gold chain, plus a cheque, which at today's value would be worth about £5,500 between them. After the inquest into his suicide, his estate was declared to be around £250,000, again by today's standards. So he wasn't in financial straits.

In those Victorian days, very few people could afford the services of a solicitor and Druitt supplemented his income by working as an assistant at George Valentine's boarding school in Blackheath. In what spare time he had, he played cricket for Blackheath, becoming their treasurer and secretary, and even played for the MCC. At the end of November 1888, he was dismissed from his school position but the reason is unclear; some speculate that he was homosexual. Could that have been at the root of his suicide? There was perhaps a genetic link causing depression. His mother had gone into an asylum, her mother and sister had committed suicide, and her eldest daughter likewise attempted suicide.

Shortly after Druitt's suicide, the police named him as one of their top three suspects. Could he have been the Ripper? Assistant Chief Constable Sir Melville Macnaghten certainly thought he was. What was the evidence?

In August 1888, Mary Ann Nichols was murdered in Whitechapel, her throat slashed. The following month, Annie Chapman, Elizabeth Stride and Catherine Eddowes were likewise found with their throats slashed. On 8th November, Mary Jane Kelly was discovered with her throat cut right back to the spine. Druitt's rooms in the Inner Temple were not far from the murder scenes. Druitt's family had a history of insanity. Druitt had committed suicide and having done so, there were no further victims. But there was other evidence which Sir Melville Macnaghten was able to produce, albeit circumstantial. A cousin of Jack Druitt had written a declaration that Jack Druitt was the

Ripper. It wasn't evidence as such but it does suggest that his own family believed it was him.

Even before the final murder, the police had observed that each one was more violent than the previous, as if the killer had to get even more gratification than the previous time. After Mary Kelly's murder, where her throat was slit right back to the spine, there was an opinion that the last one had been so violent that the killer would not be able to better it and would consequently end up in an asylum or commit suicide. From then on they monitored all asylum admissions and cases of suicides.

Sir Melville Macnaghten wasn't the only one to suggest that Jack Druitt was Jack the Ripper. In Parliament, in February 1891, Henry Farquharson, MP for West Dorset, proclaimed that the Ripper was the son of a surgeon who had committed suicide on the very night of the last murder. Whilst not naming Druitt directly, the implication was obvious.

Was Dorset's Montague John Druitt the Ripper? We shall never know but Sir Melville Macnaghten's opinion is worth recording:

> *'I have always held strong opinions regarding him, and the more I think the matter over, the stronger do these opinions become. The truth, however, will never be known, and did indeed, at one time lie at the bottom of the Thames, if my conjections be correct!"*

Keep It in the Family

It is a fact that most murders are committed by someone close to the victim, rather than by a stranger. Quite commonly that person will be an actual member of the family: a wife murdered by her husband; a jealous cousin; a bitter son. I have already mentioned Charlotte Bryant who poisoned her husband with arsenic in his Oxo; then there was Queen Elfrida who murdered her stepson for political reasons. Far more unusual, though, is the case of the granddaughter who murdered her grandfather.

She killed her grandfather

Elizabeth Marsh was just fifteen years old when she apparently committed murder. She lived with her 70-year-old grandfather in the village of Morden, not far from Poole. Little is known of what made such a young girl viciously batter her grandfather's head while he slept, there being virtually no documentary evidence, but the *Newgate Chronicle* for 1794 records the following:

> *At Dorchester Assizes, March, 1794, Elizabeth Marsh, a girl only fifteen years of age, was convicted of the murder of her grandfather, John Nevil, at Modern (sic), was condemned, and ordered to be executed forty-eight hours after.*
>
> *This girl lived with her grandfather, and, with the most deliberate malice, deprived the old man (who was seventy years of age) of his life, by giving him two dreadful blows on the head while he was asleep. This unhappy wretch was bred in such extreme ignorance that she declared she had been wholly unacquainted with the difference between good and evil, heaven and hell. She was executed according to her sentence.*

Her trial took place at the Dorchester Lent Assizes and on Friday 14th March the jury returned their verdict of guilty. The penalty was death by hanging. Under the Murder Act of 1752, executions were to take place two days after the sentence was passed. However, as that would make it a Sunday, she had an extra day of torment. There was no compassion shown. For three days she would have been kept in chains and fed on bread and water. On the day of her execution, she was taken to the gallows outside the newly-built but not yet opened Dorchester prison in North Square and was the first person to be hanged there. The execution complete, the crowd of spectators drifted away and after being left for the required hour, her body was taken down and given to local surgeons to practise dissection.

Fifteen seems a very young age to be hanging someone, especially a young girl, but elsewhere around the country, 16-year-olds were being hanged for housebreaking or shoplifting, even a 12-year-old for theft.

The murderous son-in-law

The village of Holt near Wimborne was a tight-knit farming community. Everyone knew everybody else and, generally speaking, they all got on quite well. It was into this community that, somewhere around the late 1920s, Captain Francis Burdett decided to settle, just outside Holt, at the hamlet of Dogdean. A retired army officer in his late fifties, having served in the First World War, he had a small pension but not enough to live on. He therefore supplemented this by making all kinds of ornamental leather goods and to a very high standard. Twice a year he would exhibit his work at Bournemouth and it always attracted much admiration. He boasted that he had produced commissions for the royal family and other gentry. He even renamed his bungalow *Handicraft House*.

He became a member of the local Conservative Association and put in endless hours organising events and canvassing at election times. Initially he proved very popular but, just as he seemed to be gaining acceptance, he would say something to cause offence and all the good his charm had achieved was lost in the backlash. It came to something of a head one night when he told the landlord of one of the local inns how he should be running his establishment. He was thrown out and barred. Word spread around the community and, thanks no doubt to his boastful nature, no one in the village would talk to him.

The attitude from the Holloway family at nearby Walford Farm was quite different. Thomas Holloway and his wife Louise lived there with their family, four sons and 18-year-old daughter Trixie. They felt that Burdett's treatment was quite uncharitable and, despite the risk of alienating themselves from their fellow villagers, they decided to befriend Burdett and invite him to dinner. Burdett and the family grew increasingly closer and he became a regular visitor, perhaps too regular. Young Trixie was beginning to show much interest in Burdett and his handicraft. She was invited to go to his home to view him at work. Initially it all seemed innocent but it then became apparent that the young lass was forming a strong bond with the man three times her age.

The day came when she spoke to her mother and expressed her feelings, which by now had reached the point where she had agreed to marry Burdett. Her parents were furious and forbade her to have anything more to do with the man. But Trixie's heart was set on marriage. She announced that she would be leaving the family home and moving in with Captain Burdett. Modern-day standards are far more relaxed about co-habiting but in those days between the wars, such behaviour brought disgrace to any family.

They were shocked, stunned and ashamed and did their best to persuade Trixie to return home. They even applied to the courts to issue a summons against Burdett for the abduction of a minor. The age of consent in those days was 21, not 18 as it is now. Trixie and Burdett counter-attacked with an application for court consent for their marriage. The point had been reached where the two sides could be rent apart forever unless a compromise could be reached.

Rather than lose their daughter completely and guided by the mother's wisdom, the Holloways withdrew their abduction claim and consented to their daughter's marriage. The ceremony at the register office was perhaps a sign of difficult times ahead. Apart from the couple and their witnesses, there was no one else there. At home, life wasn't much better. Money was tight and the couple struggled to survive. Trixie even had to borrow from her mother.

Matters were reaching a head. Burdett decided to visit the Holloways at their farm and beg for money. On the way he met one of the sons. It was not a friendly encounter. His request for a loan was laughed at; he was accused of being a coward and not a military hero. So aggressive was the argument, that Burdett found himself lying in the road having been punched to the ground by the angry son, who blamed Burdett for dividing the family.

Meanwhile, in Wimborne, Trixie was doing a bit of shopping. Having paid for some goods, she was asked by the proprietor if she could settle her rather large and well-overdue account. She was totally unaware of the debt and then realised that her husband had been using her good name to acquire goods. Heading for home to tackle her husband, matters got worse. Another businessman stopped her and made the same request, could she please settle her account.

When she arrived home, her husband was already there but in such a depressed mood that she felt the time was not right to tackle him. Some days later, Burdett was back at the farm, knowing that all the men folk would be out. He begged Trixie's mother to help him, for Trixie's sake. She did and lent him a fairly large sum which took the pressure off for the time being. Inevitably, the problem bounced back again and this time much worse.

During one of his depressions, Burdett had told his wife that if she returned to her family, he would shoot her. It shocked and frightened her and from then on she feared that something dreadful would happen. Days later, when out walking together they met a neighbour and Burdett asked him if he could borrow a shotgun to do a bit of hunting. Trixie was immediately suspicious of his motives. Was he planning to commit suicide?

The question was answered on 20th October 1930. Trixie was aware of her husband's restlessness through the night. He rose as daylight broke and she asked him what he was doing. Taking a stroll was his reply as he dressed and left the house. A little later, Trixie noticed that he had left a letter labelled 'Will'. Inside he had stated how he was going to put an end to it all by taking his own life. She called the police and then headed to her parents' farm to seek their help.

However, that was where Burdett himself had gone. At the farm, the family were just rising. Thomas, Trixie's father, was in her brother Alfred's room, waking him up for the milking when he heard a terrifying scream from the mother. Thomas rushed back to his wife in the bedroom and two deafening shots rang out. Alfred raced to his parents' room. He had to force the door to get it open just enough to squeeze his head in, only to be faced by the two barrels of a shotgun. Burdett was in an uncontrollable rage, threatening to kill the whole family. Alfred grabbed his brothers and got them out of the house as quickly as he could, fearing for their lives. Two of them ran to a neighbouring farm to call for help, the neighbour's son being sent to fetch the Wimborne police; the other two escaped through a barn, having been chased by Burdett.

Shortly after, the first two police officers arrived at the farm. All seemed unnaturally quiet as they entered the farmhouse. Upstairs in the bedroom they found the blood-soaked bodies of Thomas and Louise Holloway. Nearby were the two spent cartridges suggesting that Burdett had reloaded the gun. A senior police officer then arrived with the doctor, but there was nothing for him to do. The police had to focus on finding Burdett before he harmed anyone else or even himself.

They found him lying against a bank a hundred yards from the farm. The shotgun, butt end in the ground, was between his knees. Blood ran down the side of his face. He was alive but lacking the left-hand side of his face. Whilst the doctor gave him a shot of morphine, the police checked his pockets and found another four cartridges, one for each son. Theirs was a lucky escape, albeit their lives had been shattered. Two of them met Trixie as she was on her way to the farm, unaware of the disaster. They broke the news to her at which she fainted. Meanwhile, Burdett was on his way to the workhouse hospital where he died a few hours later.

At the inquest and trial, the outcome was a formality. Burdett was found guilty of murder and suicide. The jury donated their expenses to the local hospital.

The funerals of all concerned could not have provided a starker contrast. Burdett's coffin was carried on the back of a builder's wagon. At the grave side, just as the coffin was about to be lowered, there was an official objection. A suicide was about to be buried in consecrated ground and that was unacceptable. After an awkward delay, another grave was dug in an unconsecrated corner. The funeral of the two Holloways, however, was afforded the dignity the well-loved couple deserved. The churchyard was packed to capacity for their final farewell.

To My Wife, I Leave a Shilling!

Mary Brooks was born in Dorchester in May 1687, the daughter of Baptist parents Richard and Elizabeth Brooks. What sets the Baptist community apart is that children are not baptised until later in life, a fact which will become relevant later in the story. Mary's family were well-to-do and did their best to prepare her for a comfortable future. She was educated, quite literate and, in her parents' opinion, was destined to do well for herself. Mary, however, had her own ideas as to how to live her life. Perhaps she was spoilt; perhaps she was too headstrong. Certainly she was to carve her own destiny and one which would lead to her being burnt at the stake. Her mother was away from home a great deal and that could have lain at the root of her problems. Lacking maternal guidance, she became sloppy in her appearance and her speech was becoming somewhat 'common'.

The wayward daughter

Mary's parents' financial fortunes improved and, determined to achieve the best for their daughter, they packed her off first to Exeter and then to London so that she could improve herself and learn to deal with life in higher society. She was taught to dance and how to behave at social gatherings. Away from home, and her mother's guiding hand, she took advantage and found her own entertainment, visiting inns and other establishments.

Returning to Dorchester, she was a great disappointment to her parents. All the education and 'improvement' she had been provided with made no difference to her behaviour. She was soon mixing with her old friends and it was increasingly male company that she was keeping, much of it in the local inns. Not short of money, she became popular by subsidising her fellow revellers, even spending well beyond her means as she lavished her favourites with gifts.

Her extravagant behaviour, even going so far as renting houses, soon led her to steal from her parents. At the same time, she was acquiring a bad reputation amongst the finer Puritan folk of Dorchester. It should be remembered that this was just after the Monmouth Rebellion when Dorset's Puritan community rallied around the flag of the Duke of Monmouth. It was a time of high moral standards and Mary Brooks had gone well beyond the bounds of decency in her flirtatious behaviour. Her father, well aware of the rumours and accusations, did his best to persuade her to change her ways but she was having none of it. Her reaction was one of total rebellion. She declared her love for the son of a neighbour, well beneath her station in her father's opinion. Instead of calming down and backing away from the relationship, she began to go out with even more men.

She attended just about every dance going, even organising her own at the family home when her parents were away. She ordered expensive food and drinks to the embarrassment of some of her friends who knew that it had to be wrong. Well-meaning townsfolk did their best to make her parents aware of what was going on in their absence but they were reluctant to believe the stories. In desperation, they sought a way out. If they couldn't manage her behaviour, perhaps a husband could.

Marriage

Mary's father spread the word. His daughter was available for marriage and a sizeable dowry was on offer to encourage the right man to step forward. From a number of possible candidates, the competition winner was Thomas Channing, a young but well-to-do man from Maiden Newton, just eight miles away. Thomas had been set up in a grocery shop in Dorchester and his parents were as keen to see him married as were Mary's parents to see her off their hands. The problem was that Mary had her heart set in a different direction and, at each arranged meeting with Thomas, she was cold and impolite. Mary's father, along with Thomas, had realised the futility of trying to arrange the match. But they hadn't bargained for Mrs Brooks who, although not having shown much by way of maternal skills thus far, took matters into her own hands. She had Mary confined to her room until she 'came to her senses'. Mary was quite obdurate, still intending to marry the man she really loved. She persuaded a friend to contact him and ask him to rescue her by getting married to her himself. The response was not long in coming – 'No way!'.

Heartbroken and with no plan B, she conceded. She received Mr Channing in a most pleasant manner and the marriage was arranged. On 14th January 1705, after a postponement of one day due to Mary's change of heart, the couple were married. Mary then took control. She organised a party, inviting all her old friends. It was not the usual wedding celebration. She flirted with her old friends, turned her back on her husband, even ridiculing him in front of them. The situation continued day after day and the marriage became the butt of all the jokes in the district. It came as quite a shock to the parents of Thomas Channing who weren't even aware that their son had married.

She proved to be impossible as a wife. He did his best to introduce her to his circle of friends and business acquaintances but she showed them less than the respect they deserved. She stayed with her husband's uncle for a few weeks but was sent packing when he tired of her incessant chatting. Behind her husband's back, she re-acquainted herself with her former lover, pouring gifts on him and drinking with him in the local inns. In the beginning, it was done discreetly, when her husband was at church on the Sunday but she then became increasingly brazen and unashamedly continued her entertainment more openly. Channing's father, aware of what was going on and seeing how his son's finances were being frittered away, put a stop to his allowance and cut off his credit.

By the time they had been married for three months, another character entered the arena. This stranger, by the name of Nail, became her latest plaything. By way of further humiliation for her husband, she suggested that he slept somewhere else while Nail used the matrimonial bed and she would use the maid's bed!

The new will

A matter of days later, she bought poison and added it to her husband's dish of rice milk. He could only stomach a few spoonfuls before he pushed it away saying that it made him feel ill. She disposed of the evidence, flushing away what was left. Shortly after, he dashed outside and was violently sick. A neighbour's dog licked up some of the vomit and likewise was violently ill. Thomas's suspicions were aroused and he was sufficiently convinced that she was trying to poison him that he wrote a new will. In it he left all his worldly goods to his parents, with the exception of a shilling to go to his wife. The doctor was called who confirmed that he had indeed been poisoned and he left him with the appropriate medicines. Surprisingly, Mary was still allowed to attend to him and it has to be assumed that she fed him a second dose of poison, this time with fatal consequences. He died in agony.

The post mortem revealed that his body was saturated with poison. Mary, meanwhile, had disappeared from the scene. A police search of Dorchester proved fruitless. For two days she hid in a nearby village and then moved to a friend's house in woodland. Wanted posters distributed across the county offering a reward proved successful, though. The friend who had helped her to disappear, aware now of the seriousness of Mary's crime and no doubt tempted by the reward, revealed her location.

She was taken back to Dorchester and placed in the town's prison. Her trial began on 17th July 1705. She pleaded not guilty. Various witnesses were called, including Nail who had stayed at the Channing house. He described how, in the early hours of the morning, Mary Channing had entered his room, shared a bottle of drink with him and kissed him as he lay in bed – but nothing more – and she did that every morning that he stayed there. Her former lover was called and described how she gave him a gold watch even after she was married. The prosecution had already done enough to convince the jury of Mary's low moral standards. All they had to do was link her to the poison. The shopkeeper who sold her the poison testified to Mary having made the purchase. Many other witnesses were called and at the end of the three-day trial, the jury took less than half an hour to find her guilty.

Her sentence was death by execution, to be burnt at the stake. To the surprise of those present, she 'pleaded her belly'. This was a declaration of pregnancy and was often used by women to stall for time during which they hoped the death sentence would be lifted. In such cases, a team of matrons would determine her actual state. She was definitely pregnant and the execution was delayed. During that period, her mother and others of her family worked hard but unsuccessfully for a pardon. At the same time, the prison chaplain was doing his best to save her soul, ideally by confessing her sins. The best he could do was to arrange for her baptism, and that needed a special dispensation because of her refusal to admit the crime of which she had been found guilty.

Her first few weeks in prison were in relative comfort, her family paying for privileges. When the money ran out, she was moved into a small cell with no facilities. That was where her child was born on 19th December 1705 and also, despite the young age, received baptism. Mary was allowed to feed the child for its first three months and then no reason could be found to delay her execution. On 21st March, she was to be taken to Maumbury Rings, just a few minutes from Dorchester town centre.

It was a busy day on the Rings, two men were executed before it was Mary's turn. One had murdered his wife and the other was hanged for house-breaking. In football parlance, it was a game of two halves. It was a public spectacle with a large crowd. The two gentlemen having been executed, there was a short intermission while the Under Sheriff took some refreshment!

Mary's turn arrived. At five o'clock in the afternoon, she was tied to the stake. A rope went around her neck which was tightened to strangle her as the wooden faggots were quickly piled up around her. Once she was unconscious, though not yet dead, the faggots were lit and her body consumed by the flames. Whilst this may seem barbaric, we must remember that this was a different time and place. Men could be hung, drawn and quartered. The reason women were burned was because the drawing and quartering was considered ill-mannered in that it would have exposed the woman's body. It was a different culture; only fifty or sixty years earlier, witches were similarly being burned at the stake, but that's a different story.

Of Witches and Witchcraft

Witches have been around for at least two thousand years. They can still be found today, even my own grandmother would have been considered to be a witch at one time. Of course, she wasn't but she was one of those women who knew the old cures. Neighbours would come to her to have a wart removed or to be told the gender of their yet-to-be-born child; or to have their fortune told by reading the tea leaves left in the bottom of a cup; or to have their dreams explained.

The problem for witches came in 1484 when the Pope denounced witchcraft. In Dorset, as across the rest of Britain, witchcraft fever peaked in the puritanical 17th century, having been made a capital offence in 1563. The Puritans were quick to quote the Biblical statement of 'Thou shalt not suffer a witch to live'.

Dorset was always a rural county and in the 17th century the vast majority of its population were humble, agricultural folk who were of a very superstitious nature. Any unexplained event could trigger myths and rumours. Cattle giving birth to still-born calves, crops failing, a flash flood; these could all be blamed on a witch. Old women were prime suspects and once an individual had been nominated as a possible witch, almost every mishap would be blamed on her. It simply made it easy to explain the inexplicable. Those labelled as witches were undoubtedly innocent, but that didn't stop their persecution, nor did it stop the fear in which they were held in their communities.

Mummified cats

It was important to protect oneself against witchcraft and there is plenty of evidence in Dorset that demonstrates how people went about this. The museum at Portland has the remains of a mummified cat which was found in the walls of a cottage at

Easton. Mummified cats have been found elsewhere: at Corfe Mullen, Marnhull, Winfrith Newburgh and Maiden Newton. These are usually discovered with the modernisation of very old cottages when walls are removed or lofts altered. It was believed that witches could change their form, typically to become a cat or a hare, and that the best way to keep such 'familiars' out of one's house was to have another animal as a defence, hence the mummified cats. Some of these had been clubbed across the back of the neck before being walled up, others trapped in a loft where they starved to death. Hares were given the same treatment but these were hard to catch whereas cats were easy to come by.

An interesting aspect of these modern-day discoveries of witches' charms is the reaction from the house owners. We like to think that today we are not superstitious, certainly not on the same scale as 17th-century Dorset, but nonetheless these mummified cats, when discovered, are usually put back into the rebuilt wall – just in case! After all, if anything went wrong, wouldn't you have doubts about the wisdom of your decision to dispose of them?

The problem with witches was that they could so easily find their way into a home. Closing doors and windows was one way to keep them at bay, but what if they came down the chimney. The best protection for that was to take a bullock's heart, stick pins in it and shove that up the chimney. In Lyme Regis they used a chunk of bacon rather than an animal's heart. A horseshoe nailed up over a door is generally considered to bring good luck but its original purpose was to stop witches crossing the threshold.

Hag stones

For the fishermen of Dorset, the favoured protection was the use of a witch stone or hag stone. This stone is simply a smooth pebble, rounded by the action of the sea, with a natural hole at its centre. They are often found along the shore line, washed up after a storm. The hole makes it easy to use a length of rope to tie it to a fishing boat or the front door. If a fisherman was having a bad day, catching nothing when all around were catching plenty, he would reposition the hag stone around the boat until it was tuned in correctly. Dorset farming folk also tied hag stones around their horses' necks to stop witches from 'borrowing' them to ride to their ritual coven meetings. Small hag stones could be used as a pendant on a necklace and then tied to the bedpost at night. You could never be too careful.

Witch or hag stones.

Were all of these methods of keeping witches at bay really necessary? Did witches exist? They certainly did but we need to set aside any fanciful ideas of witches flying around on broomsticks or turning themselves into various forms of animals. They existed because there was something different about them and, more often than not, were simply in the wrong place at the wrong time. That was clearly the case when the Reverend William Ettrick gave Susan Woodrow the sack for being in the wrong place at the wrong time.

Sacking a witch

It was 1804. Ettrick was an intelligent fellow, well-educated and most definitely not of a superstitious nature, but that was about to change. His parish was Affpuddle and Turner's Puddle, near Bere Regis. His vicarage was quite large and required servants. In February 1804, Susan Woodrow was recruited as a gardener. She came recommended and had green fingers, able to make almost anything grow. Before she had been there a week, the vicar's horse was taken ill. There were doubts about it surviving, but then Susan was taken ill and was away for a few months. The horse recovered and she recovered, but on her return the horse was taken ill again. Over the next few months, it grew increasingly weaker, eventually failing to recover from the strangles, an infection of the airways, and died. Then an otherwise perfectly healthy pig died, rapidly followed by a dog, and then another horse which the vicar had borrowed from a neighbour.

In the November, the vicar's wife gave birth to a baby which was delivered by Susan Woodrow. From the moment of its arrival, it was in great pain and continued to be so for several days. Perhaps because his own child was involved, the vicar began to suspect Susan of being a witch. He checked the entries in his diary and realised that everything that had gone wrong had been when Susan Woodrow was present. He sent her away on some pretext and the child made a full recovery. Weeks later, Susan returned. Lo and behold, the baby was struck down again.

The vicar was now convinced that she had to be a witch but he was too afraid of her powers to do anything about it. Christmas came and went and then, having finally plucked up the courage, he sacked her, allegedly for impudence. Whatever the real reason, the household settled down to a more peaceful and healthier future.

At least the vicar had not condemned her as being a witch. In the 17th century, such an accusation would invariably have led to the accused being tried and found guilty. It was almost impossible to prove your innocence unless you died in the process, as was the case in trials by water. The accused were ducked in the river, tied to the end of a long pole. If they survived the ordeal, it was assumed that the devil had saved them and they were therefore witches. If they drowned then – whoops – they were innocent. So accusing someone of being a witch was a very dangerous thing to do. When someone accused Joanne Guppy of South Perrott of being a witch, the locals were so concerned that they signed a petition declaring her to be a good and kindly woman. The petition worked and she was spared the ordeal of a trial.

By 1884, although witches were no longer sent to trial, there was a court case in which a Mrs Tamar Humphries was in court for assaulting Sarah Smith of Sherborne for being a witch. Mrs Humphries' child had been taken ill and she was convinced that Sarah Smith, as a witch, had 'eyed' her baby. The recognised cure for such spells was to cut the witch and draw blood. Mrs Humphries had seized an opportunity and stuck a needle into Sarah Smith. The child was cured but Mrs Humphries was told by the judge not to be so superstitious and was fined for assault.

As in the case of Sarah Smith, there were many cases where an old lady was accused of casting her evil eye over some living creature. When a farmer from Milborne Port near Sherborne lost several cattle, he knew that old Mother Weller must have cast her eye over them. He also believed that you could kill a witch when she had taken the form of one of her favourite animals. In the case of Mother Weller, she was alleged to turn into a toad. When the farmer was out one night and saw a toad approaching his cattle, he stabbed it with a pitchfork. Two days later, Old Mother Weller was found dead in her bed, with a stab mark on her back!

The list goes on: Jenny Andrews of Beaminster; Deanes Gimmerton of Lyme Regis; Jane Walsh of Netherbury and many more spread right across the whole of Dorset. Are there still witches in Dorset? Of course there are but no one fears them anymore.